THE
BAPTIST FAITH & MESSAGE

Charles S. Kelley Jr.
Richard Land
R. Albert Mohler Jr.

**Learning Activities, Leader Guide, and Vignettes
of Past and Present Baptist Leaders
by Art Criscoe**

LifeWay Press®
Nashville, Tennessee

ISBN 978-1-4158-5295-8
Item 005035536

Dewey decimal classification: 230.6
Subject heading: BAPTISTS—DOCTRINES

Unless otherwise noted, Scripture quotations are taken from the Holman Christian Standard
Bible®, copyright © 1999, 2000, 2002, 2003 by Holman Bible Publishers. Used by permission. Scripture quotations marked NIV are from the Holy Bible, New International Version, copyright © 1973,
1978, 1984 by International Bible Society. Scripture quotations marked NASB are taken from the
New American Standard Bible®, Copyright © 1960, 1962, 1963, 1968, 1971, 1972, 1973, 1975,
1977, 1995 by the Lockman Foundation. Used by permission. *(www.lockman.org)*

We believe that the Bible has God for its author; salvation for its end; and truth, without any
mixture of error, for its matter and that all Scripture is totally true and trustworthy. The 2000
statement of *The Baptist Faith and Message* is our doctrinal guideline.

To order additional copies of this resource, write to LifeWay Church Resources Customer Service;
One LifeWay Plaza; Nashville, TN 37234-0113; phone toll free (800) 458-2772; fax order to (615)
251-5933; e-mail *orderentry@lifeway.com;* order online at *www.lifeway.com;* or visit the LifeWay
Christian Store serving you.

Printed in the United States of America

Leadership and Adult Publishing
LifeWay Church Resources
One LifeWay Plaza
Nashville, TN 37234-0175

CONTENTS

THE AUTHORS

Dr. Richard Land, the president of the Southern Baptist Ethics & Religious Liberty Commission, was named by *Time* in 2005 as one of America's 25 most influential evangelicals. Land has also written numerous books, including *For Faith & Family, Imagine! A God-Blessed America, Real Homeland Security,* and *The Divided States of America?* Land also hosts two nationally syndicated radio programs, "For Faith & Family" and "Richard Land Live!" *(richardlandlive.com).*

Dr. Chuck Kelley, the president of New Orleans Baptist Theological Seminary, is recognized as a passionate evangelist, preacher, and church-growth researcher. He is the author of numerous articles, training materials, and books, including *How Did They Do It? The Story of Southern Baptist Evangelism* and *The Roman Road* tract, teacher guide, and learner guide.

Dr. R. Albert Mohler Jr. is the president of the Southern Baptist Theological Seminary. He has been recognized by *Time* and *Christianity Today* as a leader among American evangelicals. Mohler hosts a daily radio program for the Salem Radio Network. He comments on moral, cultural and theological issues through his blog and online commentary. Mohler is also a contributor to *On Faith,* an online conversation about religion, sponsored by the *Washington Post* and *Newsweek* magazine. These can be accessed through his Web site, *www.albertmohler.com.*

The learning activities, leader guide, and vignettes of past and present Baptist leaders were written by Dr. Art Criscoe. Retired from LifeWay Christian Resources, Criscoe is a curriculum developer and writer for Christ to the World Ministries, an international missions organization. Criscoe has served as the pastor of churches in Texas, South Carolina, and Tennessee and as an academic dean and a professor of Bible and Christian education at Columbia Bible College in South Carolina.

DEDICATION

Adrian Rogers, 1931–2005

*Chairman, The Baptist Faith and Message Study Committee,
1999–2000*

President, Southern Baptist Convention, 1979–80, 1986–88

Adrian Rogers, denominational statesman, defender of the faith, beloved pastor, and prince among preachers is now in the presence of the Prince of Peace, having heard, "Well done, good and faithful servant" (Matt. 25:21, NIV). The world—and now heaven—will never be the same for his presence.

INTRODUCTION

Baptists are a people of deep beliefs. From the very beginning of the Baptist movement, Baptist churches and associations of churches have adopted statements of belief to teach, defend, and perpetuate the faith "that was delivered to the saints once for all" (Jude 3). These statements, most commonly known as confessions of faith, are intended to clarify and publish the most basic beliefs that frame our faith, our witness, and our worship. In the beginning years of the organized Baptist movement, these statements were often intended to demonstrate that Baptists were fully orthodox as Christian believers. Later, such statements were used to establish identity, confront false teaching, and instruct Christians in the faith.

The Southern Baptist Convention (SBC) first adopted a comprehensive statement of faith in 1925, when a committee led by E. Y. Mullins presented *The Baptist Faith and Message* to the Convention. The statement was a revised edition of the New Hampshire Confession of Faith, then commonly used by Baptists in both the North and the South.

The 1925 committee brought its report during an era of controversy in Baptist life. The fundamentalist/modernist controversy raged in northern denominations, and a growing climate of antisupernaturalism in the larger culture fueled Southern Baptist concern. Another period of controversy emerged in the early 1960s over the nature and authority of Scripture, and Southern Baptists revised

The Baptist Faith and Message in 1963 at the recommendation of a committee led by Herschel Hobbs.

That committee revised the 1925 statement considerably, though it also explained, "In no case [have we] sought to delete from or to add to the basic contents of the 1925 Statement." The 1963 statement added new articles and revised the language and content of the 1925 statement in significant areas. New concerns and emerging challenges led the Southern Baptists of that era to revise *The Baptist Faith and Message* and to clarify our common beliefs.

The SBC affirmed *The Baptist Faith and Message* in subsequent conventions, and in 1969 it adopted a motion encouraging the agencies, boards, and institutions of the Convention to use *The Baptist Faith and Message* as a guideline in employment, editorial content, and policy.

The Baptist Faith and Message was next revised in 1998, when the SBC adopted "Article 18: The Family" at its meeting in Salt Lake City, Utah, in the midst of widespread societal concern about the breakdown of the family. The next year the SBC adopted a motion calling on the president of the Convention to appoint a committee to review *The Baptist Faith and Message* and to bring a report and any recommendations to the Convention meeting the following year.[1]

The Baptist Faith and Message Study Committee, with Adrian Rogers as the chairman, brought its report and recommendations to the SBC meeting in Orlando, Florida, in June 2000. During that meeting the Convention adopted the report, including a revised version of *The Baptist Faith and Message*.

Looking back to the 1925 statement, Herschel Hobbs remarked, "This statement served in large measure to anchor Southern Baptists to their traditional theological moorings for a generation." In reality, each new generation must reclaim the priceless doctrinal heritage. At the dawn of a new millennium, *The Baptist Faith and Message* now serves to anchor this generation of Baptists to those same theological moorings.

We were honored to serve on *The Baptist Faith and Message* Study Committee, and we are honored to present this commentary to our fellow Southern Baptists. Our prayer is that God will lead this generation of Southern Baptists into a bold new era of missions, evangelism, ministry, and vision and that God will bless our witness to His truth through *The Baptist Faith and Message*.

1. Members of the committee included Max Barnett (OK), Steve Gaines (AL), Susie Hawkins (TX), Rudy A. Hernandez (TX), Charles S. Kelley Jr. (LA), Heather King (IN), Richard Land (TN), Fred Luter (LA), R. Albert Mohler Jr. (KY), T. C. Pinckney (VA), Nelson Price (GA), Adrian Rogers (chairman, TN), Roger Spradlin (CA), Simon Tsoi (AZ), and Jerry Vines (FL).

CHAPTER 1

THE SCRIPTURES

Article 1

The Scriptures

"The Holy Bible was written by men divinely inspired and is God's revelation of Himself to man. It is a perfect treasure of divine instruction. It has God for its author, salvation for its end, and truth, without any mixture of error, for its matter. Therefore, all Scripture is totally true and trustworthy. It reveals the principles by which God judges us, and therefore is, and will remain to the end of the world, the true center of Christian union, and the supreme standard by which all human conduct, creeds, and religious opinions should be tried. All Scripture is a testimony to Christ, who is Himself the focus of divine revelation."[1]

> **Memory Verses**
>
> "All Scripture is inspired by God and is profitable for teaching, for rebuking, for correcting, for training in righteousness, so that the man of God may be complete, equipped for every good work." 2 Timothy 3:16-17

Southern Baptists are known as a people of the Book. That Book is the Bible. We come from all walks of life. With more than 16 million members, our churches number more than 43,000 and dot the landscape. Spread from sea to sea, we are found in every state. Some of us worship in small country churches, and some of us meet in large city churches. Included in our number are churches that meet in huge, arena-type settings and churches that meet in portable buildings. Common to all of us, however, is our love for the Bible.

God's Revelation

When we speak of the Bible or the Holy Scriptures, we are talking about 66 books divided into the Old and New Testaments. This Book is different from any other book, for it is not a collection of human opinions about God but is in fact God's own Word. Baptists love and respect the Bible as the Word of God.

As God's written revelation of Himself to humankind, the Bible is one of God's most precious gifts to us. In His written Word God has spoken to His people, taking the initiative to reveal Himself to us and to disclose Himself in a very real and understandable way. Without this divine self-disclosure we would have no certain knowledge of God, and all humanity would be left groping for answers in the dark. Each individual would have his or her own idea about God's existence, character, and expectations of us. God's revelation is a beautiful demonstration of His love for us. He did not leave us in the dark.

The Bible acknowledges that God has revealed Himself to all humanity through creation itself. As the psalmist reminds us,

General Revelation
God's making known His nature and purpose through nature and history

Special Revelation
God's making known His nature and purpose through the written Word and His Son Jesus Christ

> The heavens declare the glory of God,
> and the sky proclaims the work of His hands.
> Psalm 19:1

Every atom and molecule of creation reveals the wonder of God's marvelous design. The intricate balance of creation, the beauty of the earth and its varied landscapes, the wonder of a sunset—all these declare God's greatness and glory. Beyond this, God reveals Himself to all persons through the moral faculty we call conscience. Our undeniable knowledge of good and evil, of right and wrong, points us to the perfect moral character of our Creator. These types of revelation, which God gave to all people who have ever lived, are called general revelation or natural revelation. God's revelation of Himself through the Bible and through His Son Jesus Christ is called special revelation.

Identify each item as special revelation (S) or general revelation (G) by placing the correct letter in each blank.
___ 1. The beauty of creation ___ 4. The Book of Isaiah
___ 2. The conscience within ___ 5. Mountains, rivers
___ 3. The Bible ___ 6. John 3:16

Read Romans 1:20 in the margin. Check below two things we can learn about God from what He has created.
☐ God's love through Christ ☐ God's divine nature
☐ God's power of God ☐ The work of the Holy Spirit

Items 1, 2, and 5 are general revelation, while 3, 4, and 6 are special revelation. God's creation reveals His power and divine nature.

If general revelation is available to all people, why do we need the Bible? The Apostle Paul answered this question by explaining that our sin blinds us to a full understanding of God's revelation of Himself in nature and in our conscience. As he wrote to the Christians in Rome, human beings "exchanged the truth of God for a lie, and worshiped and served something created instead of the Creator" (Rom. 1:25). Our sin so distorts our spiritual vision that we love the lie and hate the truth. God graciously provided humankind special revelation through His divine Word to teach us more about His nature, His redemptive purpose, and His will for our lives.

"From the creation of the world His invisible attributes, that is, His eternal power and divine nature, have been clearly seen, being understood through what He has made. As a result, people are without excuse."
Romans 1:20

God for Its Author

The Bible is God's revelation of Himself to humanity, and God is rightly known as the Author of all Scripture. Charles Haddon Spurgeon (1834–92), one of the greatest preachers in Christian history, said in a sermon in 1855, "This volume is the writing of the living God. ... everywhere I find God speaking: it is God's voice, not man's;

the words are God's words, the words of the Eternal, the Invisible, the Almighty, the Jehovah of this earth. This Bible is God's Bible; and when I see it, I seem to hear a voice springing up from it, saying, 'I am the book of God: man, read me.' "[2]

As *The Baptist Faith and Message* affirms, the Bible was written by men divinely inspired. What does this mean? We commonly hear that a particular human author like William Shakespeare was inspired. After an especially moving musical performance, someone may remark that the composer or performer was inspired. Is the Bible inspired in this same way?

Inspiration
The breathing of God's Spirit on human speech and writing to produce the text of the Bible

Of course not. If the Bible were merely a collection of particularly insightful writings about God, we would not stake our lives on its truth. Some have erroneously taught that the Bible is merely the product of an elevated human consciousness. Others have suggested that the Bible is unevenly inspired. Some parts, they argue, are more inspired than other parts. This view places the human reader over Scripture as judge, deciding what parts are most inspired and what parts can be ignored or denied.

Other people have argued that God merely inspired the ideas contained in the Bible, not the words of Scripture itself. This *dynamic* theory of the Bible's inspiration holds that God gave the human authors basic ideas that they developed in their own ways. At the other extreme is the *dictation* theory, which sees the human authors as passive instruments of the Holy Spirit's inspiration, simply taking down divine dictation for the record.

Like today, more than one hundred years ago Baptists were confronted with such theories of biblical inspiration. Basil Manly Jr. (1825–92) was one of the four founding faculty members of the Southern Baptist Theological Seminary in 1859 and taught at the seminary for many years.[3] Manly's seminary colleagues asked him to respond to dangerous theories that were infecting some churches, seminaries, and denominations. After reviewing the false theories of inspiration, Manly summarized an understanding of the full inspiration of the Scriptures with these words: "The Bible as a whole is the Word of God, so that in every part of Scripture there is both infallible truth and divine authority."[4] This is the conclusion of the *verbal plenary* theory of the Bible's inspiration. Put simply, this means that the Bible's inspiration is *verbal*—extending to the very words themselves—and *plenary*, or full. Thus, we affirm that *every* word of the Bible is inspired and that every word is *fully* inspired.

Match each theory of inspiration with its definition by placing the correct letter in each blank.

C 1. The dynamic theory

b 2. The verbal plenary theory

a 3. The dictation theory

a. The authors were passive instruments who recorded divine dictation.

b. Every word of the Bible is fully inspired.

c. God gave human authors basic ideas that they developed in their own ways.

"It [the Bible] is a great revelation of the will of God. It is divinely inspired, every book and chapter and verse and word of it."[5]

M. E. Dodd
1878–1952
Pastor, First Baptist Church; Shreveport, Louisiana; president, Southern Baptist Convention, 1934–35

The answers are 1. c, 2. b, 3. a.

We believe the verbal plenary theory expresses the way the Bible describes its own inspiration. The Bible's word for its inspiration is *God-breathed* (see 2 Tim. 3:16-17). The Holy Spirit breathed this Word through human authors divinely chosen for this task. God used their personalities, writing styles, and personal experiences to accomplish His perfect purpose. These human authors were not passive stenographers; rather, the Holy Spirit worked through them, inspiring them so thoroughly that they were moved to write exactly what God intended—right down to the very words. As the Bible records, the will and initiative were God's own, "because no prophecy ever came by the will of man; instead, moved by the Holy Spirit, men spoke from God" (2 Pet. 1:21). The result of divine inspiration is that we have exactly the Bible God intends for us to have. Nothing is missing. Nothing is included that should not be there. For this reason we affirm that the Bible is the very Word of God and does not merely contain the Word

"All Scripture is God-breathed and is useful for teaching, rebuking, correcting and training in righteousness, so that the man of God may be thoroughly equipped for every good work."
2 Timothy 3:16-17, NIV

"When God super-naturally directed the writers of Scripture, He did not suspend their personalities, literary styles, or emotions. But He communicated His truth by guiding their thoughts, guarding them from error, and producing a totally reliable message. Thus, every word of the original manuscripts bears the authority of divine authorship. This means that the Bible is accurate in all it says, and it does not deceive its readers theologically, historically, chronologically, geographically, or scientifically."[7]

James T. Draper Jr.
1935–
President emeritus, LifeWay Christian Resources; president, Southern Baptist Convention, 1982–84

of God. God speaks to us through His Word, and where the Scripture speaks, God speaks.

Belief in the Bible as the very Word of God has been the conviction of Baptists through the years. John L. Dagg (1794–1884), a pastor, teacher, and administrator, wrote, "The men who spoke and wrote as they were moved by the Holy Ghost were the instruments that God used to speak and write His word. Their peculiarities of thought, feeling, and style, had no more effect to prevent what they spoke and wrote from being the word of God, than their peculiarities of voice or of chirography [penmanship]. The question, whether inspiration extended to the very words of revelation, as well as to the thoughts and reasonings, is answered by Paul: 'We preach, not in the *words* which man's wisdom teacheth, but which the Holy Ghost teacheth.' "[6]

Mark each statement *T* (true) or *F* (false).

___ 1. We have exactly the Bible God intends for us to have.

___ 2. God guided the writers of Scripture to produce His truth.

___ 3. Some parts of the Bible are more inspired than other parts.

___ 4. God gave the writers of Scripture basic ideas that they developed in their own ways.

___ 5. The Bible does not deceive us in any way.

___ 6. God used the personalities, writing styles, and life experiences of the authors of Scripture to accomplish His perfect purpose.

Statements 1, 2, 5, and 6 are true; statements 3 and 4 are false.

A lifelong trust in the Bible as the Word of God characterized the life of W. A. Criswell (1909–2002). When he was a student at Baylor University, he had a friend who withdrew from the Christian faith and became a skeptic. He told Criswell that the Bible was just another book. Criswell said to his friend, "I know the Bible isn't always easy to understand, but I will never end up treating the Bible like any other book. It is the Word of God. The universe is sustained by His Word.

We are convicted and converted through it. The Word keeps us from sin. We walk by it, live by it and one day we'll die by it. Our assurance of heaven is only through the Word. Understand it all or not, like it all or not, the Word is the foundation of life, and without it our souls wither up and die."[8]

Criswell eventually became the pastor of First Baptist Church in Dallas, Texas, which grew to 28,000 members under his preaching. After a lifetime in the ministry, Criswell wrote at 90 years of age, "This I believe and this I proclaim: God's Word is perfect, literal, inerrant, infallible, and totally trustworthy."[9]

Salvation for Its End

Because the Bible is the uniquely inspired Word of God, it is a perfect treasure of divine instruction. Every word is to be trusted and obeyed. Time and time again, God reminded His people that He gave us this Word so that we could have life and be faithful to Him.

Speaking through Moses, God repeatedly instructed the children of Israel that His Word was to be obeyed for their good and that disobedience would lead to death and disaster. Read Deuteronomy 6:1-2 in the margin. The formula presented in these verses is very easy to understand: obedience to God's Word leads to life and blessing; disobedience leads to catastrophe.

The Bible is our authoritative guide to God's truth and is the sure foundation on which to build our lives and stake our hopes. As the psalmist declared,

> Your word is a lamp for my feet
> and a light on my path.
> Psalm 119:105

A Christian loves the Word of God and demonstrates this love by obeying it and by being faithful in personal Bible study. A church demonstrates a hunger for the Bible by its desire and support for true biblical preaching and teaching. Nothing less will do; no substitute can satisfy our hunger for the Word of God.

"This is the command— the statutes and ordinances—the Lord your God has instructed me to teach you, so that you may follow them in the land you are about to enter and possess. Do this so that you may fear the Lord your God all the days of your life by keeping all His statutes and commands I am giving you, your son, and your grandson, and so that you may have a long life."
Deuteronomy 6:1-2

State at least three ways believers can demonstrate a love for the Word of God.

1. _____

2. _____

3. _____

We can show our love for God's Word by diligently studying it, by obeying it, by listening to biblical preaching and teaching, by sharing its truths, and other ways.

As God's Word, the Bible is fully able to accomplish all God intends for it to do. In Hebrews the Bible is described as "living and effective and sharper than any two-edged sword" (4:12). Through the prophet Isaiah God declared that

> My word that comes from My mouth
> will not return to Me empty,
> but it will accomplish what I please,
> and will prosper in what I send it to do.
> Isaiah 55:11

Paul reminded Timothy that "all Scripture is inspired by God and is profitable for teaching, for rebuking, for correcting, for training in righteousness, so that the man of God may be complete, equipped for every good work" (2 Tim. 3:16-17). Thus, God promises to work through His Word to accomplish these good things in us, both individually and corporately in the church. Furthermore, this text promises that Christians are shaped into maturity by the power of the Word so that we are equipped for every good work.

The absence or neglect of God's Word is a scandal in any generation, but we can see the devastating loss that comes to churches, denominations, families, and individual lives when God's Word is ignored, distorted, or disobeyed. The absence of God's Word leads to death.

This truth serves as a powerful reminder that the primary purpose of the Bible is to tell how to be saved. This is what *The Baptist Faith and Message* means in saying that the Bible has "salvation for its end." The Apostle John insisted on this purpose when he told his readers,

"I have been studying, preaching, teaching, and writing about the New Testament for over fifty years. But I never open my Greek New Testament without finding something I had never before seen in it."[10]

A. T. Robertson
1863–1934
Professor, the Southern Baptist Theological Seminary

"I have written these things to you who believe in the name of the Son of God, so that you may know that you have eternal life" (1 John 5:13).

The Bible—God's written Word—fulfills God's redemptive goal by pointing us to Jesus Christ, the incarnate Word. Jesus is the ultimate focus of every verse of Scripture, and as He explained, "You pore over the Scriptures because you think you have eternal life in them, yet they testify about Me" (John 5:39). The Scriptures find their fulfillment in Christ and reveal the salvation that comes by faith in Him.

> Jesus is the ultimate focus of every verse of Scripture.

Jesus Christ is the ultimate revelation of God, but we would have no authoritative knowledge of Him apart from the Bible. The written Word and the incarnate Word must never be seen in contradiction or competition with each other. A division between Christ and the Bible is a sure sign of false teaching. Christ is honored when the Bible is taught, preached, and believed.

The primary purpose of the Bible is to (choose one)—
    ☐ teach us the Golden Rule;
    ☐ warn us about false religions;
    ☐ tell us how to be saved;
    ☐ help us face the problems of life.

In the previous paragraphs underline at least three other purposes of Scripture.

The main purpose of the Bible is to point us to Jesus Christ and to tell us how to be saved. Other purposes include teaching, rebuking, correcting, training in righteousness, and equipping for good works.

Truth Without Any Mixture of Error

Can we really trust the Bible? If the Bible contained error, how could we trust it? We would be left in an endless debate about which parts of the Bible are true and trustworthy and which parts are not. How could we stake our lives on a fallible revelation?

Early in Billy Graham's ministry he became troubled when a close friend and coworker turned away from belief in the Bible as the inspired Word of God. The friend ridiculed Graham for believing the

"If you read the Old Testament, you will find phrases like 'the Word of the Lord' or 'the Word of God' or 'God spoke' or 'the Lord said' used 3,808 times. If the Bible is not the Word of God, it's the biggest bundle of lies that has ever come to planet Earth. The Bible is truth, absolutely."[14]

Adrian Rogers
1931–2005
Pastor, Bellevue Baptist Church; Memphis, Tennessee; president, Southern Baptist Convention, 1979–80, 1986–88

Bible. The question, Is the Bible completely true? constantly nagged Graham until it reached a crisis point at a retreat center in the San Bernardino Mountains in August 1949. He walked into the woods one night with his Bible, opened it and placed it on a tree stump, knelt before it, and poured out his thoughts to God. He concluded his prayer by saying, "Father, I am going to accept this as Thy Word—by *faith!* I'm going to allow faith to go beyond my intellectual questions and doubts, and I will believe this to be Your inspired Word."[11] As he returned to his room, he sensed God's presence and power in a new way. The experience was a turning point for young Graham. "In my heart and mind, I knew a spiritual battle in my soul had been fought and won."[12]

The Los Angeles crusade began in a few weeks, and Graham began a lifelong ministry of worldwide evangelism. As he preached in crowded stadiums around the word, his sermons were punctuated with "The Bible says. ..." He never veered from his experience with God in the mountains of California. Graham wrote in 2006 at 87 years of age, "As I grow older, my confidence in the inspiration and authority of the Bible has grown even stronger."[13]

The Baptist Faith and Message has always stated that the Bible is "truth, without any mixture of error," affirming without qualification the absolute perfection of the Holy Scriptures. Just as God is perfect, His Word is perfect. The psalmist put this conviction to song:

> The instruction of the LORD is perfect, reviving the soul;
> the testimony of the LORD is trustworthy, making the inexperienced wise.
> Psalm 19:7

We should give careful attention to five specific ways Baptists affirm that the Bible is "truth, without any mixture of error." The Bible is authoritative, infallible, inerrant, sufficient, and eternal.

The Bible is authoritative. The essential meaning of this word is found in its root. We recognize the Bible's authority because we recognize God as its author. If God is the author of the Scriptures, every word of the

Bible bears God's own authority. Christians have no right to dismiss or question any biblical text, for all Scripture is God-breathed.

Baptists recognize the Bible's authority by drawing all we do and teach and preach directly from the biblical text. Christ rules in His church through the ministry of the Word. We find all true doctrine in the Word of God, decide all doctrinal controversies by the Bible, and discover what it means to be a disciple of Christ by living the teachings of the Bible. We do not base our teachings on mere human tradition, nor do we base our faith on human wisdom. The Bible, and the Bible alone, is the rule for our faith and life.

The Bible is infallible. God never fails, nor does His Word. We can trust that the Bible will always accomplish God's purposes (see Isa. 55:11). It is the strongest weapon in the hands of a believer (see Eph. 6:17). Human wisdom will fail, as will human witnesses, but the Word of God never fails.

> "Take ... the sword of the Spirit, which is God's word."
> Ephesians 6:17

Some have used the concept of the Bible's infallibility to limit the reach of its truthfulness. They argue that the Bible is infallible only in that it accomplishes its purpose of telling us of salvation. On that matter it is to be trusted, they say, but not when the Bible speaks of other issues. This notion of limited infallibility is seductive but very dangerous. If the Bible cannot be trusted in all it teaches, how can we have confidence that it can be trusted in any of its teachings?

The Bible is inerrant. The Bible is truth—all truth—and contains no error of any kind. In a hallway at LifeWay Christian Resources in Nashville, Tennessee, hangs a plaque with this inscription: "We accept the Scriptures as an all-sufficient and infallible rule of faith and practice, and insist upon the absolute inerrancy and sole authority of the Word of God."[15] The author of these words, J. M. Frost (1848–1916), led the denomination to establish the Sunday School Board in 1891 to provide biblically sound literature for churches to use in teaching and training, and he served as the agency's first general secretary.

Inerrancy has been a controversial word in some circles, and some Baptists have argued that this word is unnecessary and divisive. Why is it so important to affirm that the Bible is "truth, without any mixture

"When I was a boy I thought I had found a thousand contradictions in the Bible. ... I do not see them now; they are not there. There are perhaps a half dozen in the Bible that I cannot explain satisfactorily to myself. ... Since I have seen nine hundred and ninety-four out of the thousand coalesce and harmonize like two streams mingling, I am disposed to think that if I had more sense I could harmonize those other six."[16]

B. H. Carroll
1843–1914
Founder, Southwestern Baptist Theological Seminary

of error"? The real issue is not the word but the concept it conveys. To reject the inerrancy of the Bible is to assert that some error must be present. What kind of error? Where is it found? The affirmation of the Bible's inerrancy is directly connected to its inspiration, infallibility, and authority. We can be confident that the Holy Spirit fully inspired every word of the Bible in its original text. Because God is the Bible's ultimate Author, a denial of inerrancy denies His perfection and undermines the Bible's authority. It is also inconsistent to claim that the Bible can be infallible in its purpose while containing errors, no matter how small.

One of the simplest and most profound statements of the Bible's perfection came from Jesus Himself. On the night of His betrayal, He prayed to the Father for His church with these words:

Sanctify them by the truth;
Your word is truth.
John 17:17

One of the first messages the resurrected Christ spoke to His disciples on the road to Emmaus was to believe "all that the prophets have spoken" (Luke 24:25).

The Bible is sufficient. We are not to add to the Bible or to subtract from it. God warned His people in unmistakable terms, "You must not add anything to what I command you or take anything away from it, so that you may keep the commands of the LORD your God I am giving you" (Deut. 4:2). Relying on the wisdom of God found in the Bible, we are warned not to turn to the wisdom of the world. Our minds are to be captive to the Word of God, deciding all issues from biblical wisdom. This means that a Christian worldview based on the Bible will necessarily conflict with worldviews based on human wisdom.

As *The Baptist Faith and Message* explains, this is why the Bible is "the true center of Christian union, and the supreme standard by which all human conduct, creeds, and religious opinions should be tried." Where else would we turn?

The Bible is eternal. This is true simply because God is eternal. Peter explained this truth by quoting the Old Testament prophet Isaiah (see 1 Pet. 1:24-25 in the margin). This truth was vividly illustrated during the time of Jeremiah. The prophet lived and preached during the final days before his nation was overthrown by Babylon. Around 604 B.C. God commanded the prophet to write His words on a scroll. When king Jehoiakim learned about the scroll, he ordered that it be brought and read before him. The king was seated before an open fire as the servant read God's Word. "As soon as Jehudi would read three or four columns, Jehoiakim would cut the scroll with a scribe's knife and throw the columns into the blazing fire until the entire scroll was consumed by the fire in the brazier" (Jer. 36:23).

> "All flesh is like grass, and all its glory like a flower of the grass. The grass withers, and the flower drops off, but the word of the Lord endures forever."
> 1 Peter 1:24-25

Jehoiakim soon learned what enemies of Bible have discovered through the centuries: God's Word cannot be destroyed. "The word of the Lord came to Jeremiah: 'Take another scroll, and once again write on it the very words that were on the original scroll that Jehoiakim king of Judah burned' " (Jer. 36:27-28).

The Bible is not a passing deposit of divine revelation. It cannot be superseded by another word or revelation. Ultimately, it is completely fulfilled in Jesus Christ, the incarnate Word, and its truth endures forever.

Following are five terms used to describe the Bible.
Match each term with the correct definition.

___ 1. Authoritative
___ 2. Infallible
___ 3. Inerrant
___ 4. Sufficient
___ 5. Eternal

a. The Bible is all truth and contains no errors of any kind.
b. God's Word will endure forever.
c. Every word of the Bible bears God's own authority.
d. God's Word never fails.
e. We are to rely on God's wisdom found in the Bible rather than the world's wisdom.

The correct answers are 1. c, 2. d, 3. a, 4. e, 5. b.

The Baptist Faith and Message does not begin with the Scriptures by mere accident or custom. Where else would we begin? God has spoken, and He has given us His Word in the Bible. All of the other doctrines we will study in this book are truths found in God's Word.

"Dear God, I commit to reading a portion of Your Word each day. Please help me keep this commitment and learn what You want to teach me through Your Word. In Jesus' name."

_____
SIGNED

_____
DATE

One way to show appreciation for and trust in the Bible as God's Word is to read it each day. Consider signing the prayer in the margin as an affirmation to God that you will begin or continue reading the Bible each day.

God has promised to bless us when we meditate on His Word. Consider meditating on your memory verses for this chapter, 2 Timothy 3:16-17, each day this week. Here are suggestions for meditating.

1. Commit to 15 minutes each day.
2. Select a special place and time to meet with God.
3. Begin by praying Psalm 19:14.
4. Slowly read the verses in an open, humble, and loving manner. Read them audibly and repeatedly, letting the verses speak to your mind and heart.
5. Meditate on the passage. Think of the meaning of each word and each phrase. Let the passage saturate your being. Acknowledge in your heart the greatness and holiness of the loving God who gave His Word.
6. Pray, thanking God for the truths in the passage. Pray the verse back to God. Your prayer may include adoration, confession, thanksgiving, and supplication or petition. Periods of silence are appropriate.
7. Write the verses on a small card and carry it with you. Read them and reflect on them during the week.[17]

CHAPTER 2
GOD

Article 2

God

"There is one and only one living and true God. He is an intelligent, spiritual, and personal Being, the Creator, Redeemer, Preserver, and Ruler of the universe. God is infinite in holiness and all other perfections. God is all powerful and all knowing; and His perfect knowledge extends to all things, past, present, and future, including the future decisions of His free creatures. To Him we owe the highest love, reverence, and obedience. The eternal triune God reveals Himself to us as Father, Son, and Holy Spirit, with distinct personal attributes, but without division of nature, essence, or being."[1]

> **Memory Verse**
>
> "Do not have other gods besides Me." Exodus 20:3

Knowing God is the highest privilege given to humanity.

The most important and urgent knowledge humans can ever possess is the knowledge of the one true and living God. This is the beginning and end of all genuine knowledge, and knowing God is the highest privilege given to humanity. In addition, the knowledge of God is the foundation of the Christian worldview, setting it apart from all other worldviews. Our concept of God and our belief that He exists make all the difference in the way we look at the world and live our lives.

At the same time, we must be very careful to make certain that our knowledge of God is based solidly on the Bible and not on human speculation. Why is this a concern? Researchers indicate that only a bare fraction of Americans are atheists or agnostics. If you took this fact at face value, you would think that America must be experiencing a great revival and spiritual recovery. This is hardly the case.

The sad truth is that many Americans have only a superficial idea of God. The God they imagine is not the living God of the Bible but more the product of sentimentality. Human wisdom does not reveal God's true nature, nor can the human imagination even come close to His glory. True wisdom comes by knowing God as He has revealed Himself in the Scriptures. As God spoke through the prophet Jeremiah,

> The wise must not boast in his wisdom;
> the mighty must not boast in his might;
> the rich must not boast in his riches.
> But the one who boasts should boast in this,
> that he understands and knows Me.
> Jeremiah 9:23-24

The highest aspiration of the human soul and mind must be to know the one true and living God, to enjoy Him, and to serve Him with gladness.

One Living and True God

The Baptist Faith and Message states the most important first step in knowing God: "There is one and only one living and true God." The words *one and only one* express a point about which God Himself is very particular and insistent. He is not one among other gods or even the greatest among all other gods. He is the only true God. God made this point very powerfully through Isaiah when He declared,

> I am the LORD, and there is no other;
> there is no God but Me.
> Isaiah 45:5

As the children of Israel prepared to enter the land of promise, Moses instructed them, "Listen, Israel: The LORD our God, the LORD is One" (Deut. 6:4). In the New Testament Paul taught this same truth to the Corinthians: "We know that 'an idol is nothing in the world,' and that 'there is no God but one'" (1 Cor. 8:4). E. Y. Mullins explained this truth by noting, "The doctrine of many gods is polytheism, and against it the prophets of the Old Testament poured out their inspired and burning eloquence. The Old Testament is the record of how God trained Israel to the thought of a pure monotheism, that is, to the belief in one holy and spiritual God."[2]

The Attributes of God

God is intelligent, spiritual, and personal. By *intelligent* we affirm that God is a knowing Being, not a blind force. Not only is He knowing, but He is also all-knowing or, as God described Himself, He has "perfect knowledge" (Job 37:16). At best our human knowledge is partial. God's knowledge is infinite. By *spiritual* we affirm that God is a transcendent Being who is in no way limited by a physical body. As Jesus told the woman at the well, "God is spirit, and those who worship Him must worship in spirit and truth" (John 4:24). By *personal* we affirm that God has a personality and relates to His people in a personal way (see Ezek. 34:24,30-31). The fact that He is personal makes it possible for us to relate to Him (see Ps. 86:1-7; 116:1-2).

God is self-existent, self-sufficient, and eternal. He depends on nothing and is complete in Himself. The only uncreated being, God made all things and brought all creatures into being (see Gen. 1:1). He is eternal (see Isa. 57:15). There never was a time when He was not, there never will be a time when He is not, and He Himself is the Creator of time.

"I, the LORD, will be their God, and My servant David will be a prince among them. I, the LORD, have spoken. Then they will know that I, the LORD their God, am with them, and that they, the house of Israel, are My people. This is the declaration of the Lord God. You are My flock, the human flock of My pasture, and I am your God."
Ezekiel 34:24,30-31

23

When Moses asked His name, God responded, "I AM WHO I AM" (Ex. 3:14). His name establishes His eternality and self-existence.

God is glorious. Although God does not need His creatures, He chooses to glorify Himself through them. Our God is a God of glory. The Bible is filled with passages about the glory of God—the radiance of His deity and the shining reflection of His majesty (see Num. 16:42; 1 Chron. 16:28-29; 29:11; Ps. 19:1; 24:7-8; 72:19; 96:3; Rom. 11:36; Rev. 4:11). There is no one like Him and no one to whom He can be compared. The more we know Him, the more we see His glory, and the more perfectly we glorify Him.

God is unchanging. Unlike us, God never changes. As the great hymn resounds, "There is no shadow of turning"[3] in Him; He is not forced to change His will or His ways (see 1 Sam. 15:29). God's being is unchanging. He is never greater or lesser than He was before. His character is also unchanging, a fact that is a great comfort to His people (see Mal. 3:6). Our God is not quick to anger (see Num. 14:18), and He keeps His promises (see 1 Kings 8:56; Jer. 33:14).

> "Declare His glory among the nations, His wonderful works among all peoples."
> Psalm 96:3

> "From Him and through Him and to Him are all things. To Him be the glory forever."
> Romans 11:36

> "Because I, Yahweh, have not changed, you descendants of Jacob have not been destroyed."
> Malachi 3:6

Match each attribute of God with its description.

___ 1. Unchanging

___ 2. Spiritual

___ 3. All-knowing

___ 4. Eternal

___ 5. Self-existent

___ 6. Personal

a. There never was a time when God was not.

b. God is complete in Himself; He needs nothing.

c. God keeps His promises.

d. God's knowledge is infinite.

e. God is not limited to a physical body.

f. God relates to His people in a personal way.

You should have matched the attributes this way: 1. c, 2. e, 3. d, 4. a, 5. b, 6. f.

The Activity of God

The Bible tells us that God is the Creator, Redeemer, Preserver, and Ruler of the universe. These terms help us understand the comprehensive nature of God's relationship with the created order. This understanding is foundational to our confidence that God is in control of history and creation.

God is Creator. God brought all things into being by the power of His word (see Gen. 1). He did not fashion the world out of preexisting matter; He created all things *ex nihilo*—out of nothing. Until God created the world and everything in it, nothing existed at all. After creating the world, God declared it to be good (see Gen. 1), and all of creation ultimately exists for His glory (see Ps. 19:1).

God is Redeemer. God rescues His people from peril. In the Old Testament He redeemed Israel from bondage to the Egyptians (see Ex. 6–12) and promised a more perfect redemption to come. The New Testament tells the story of God's redeeming love as revealed and fulfilled by Jesus Christ.

God is Preserver. God protects and guards His creation and His creatures. No creature, no matter how small, escapes His concern and care. As Jesus taught His disciples, not even a sparrow falls without His concern (see Matt. 10:29). No atom or molecule of matter is beyond His care and concern.

God is Ruler. God exercises His kingly lordship over the entire cosmos. As the Bible makes clear, God remains intimately involved with His creation. Christianity is incompatible with deism, the belief that God created the world only to withdraw from it, merely observing its unfolding history. On the contrary, God always remains the Ruler of all He has made (see 1 Chron. 29:11-12; Dan. 4:17).

Because God is Ruler, we owe Him the highest love, reverence, and obedience. The very fact that God allows us to know and to love Him is a sign of His loving character. Reverence naturally flows from the acknowledgment that He is our Creator and Redeemer. We revere

> "The heavens declare the glory of God, and the sky proclaims the work of His hands."
> Psalm 19:1

> "Yours, LORD, is the greatness and the power and the glory and the splendor and the majesty, for everything in the heavens and on earth belongs to You. Yours, LORD, is the kingdom, and You are exalted as head over all. Riches and honor come from You, and You are the ruler of everything. In Your hand are power and might, and it is in Your hand to make great and to give strength to all."
> 1 Chronicles 29:11-12

25

Him by honoring His name and respecting His Word. In addition, God as Ruler demands to be obeyed. As Moses instructed the children of Israel, "Carefully observe the commands of the LORD your God, the decrees and statutes He has commanded you" (Deut. 6:17).

Read each Scripture and match the reference with the activity of God to which it refers.

___ 1. Psalm 147:9	a. Ruler
___ 2. Psalm 66:7	b. Preserver
___ 3. Exodus 15:18	c. Creator
___ 4. John 1:3	d. Redeemer
___ 5. Jeremiah 32:17	
___ 6. Colossians 1:17	
___ 7. Titus 2:14	
___ 8. Job 19:25	

The correct answers are 1. b, 2. a, 3. a, 4. c, 5. c, 6. b, 7. d, 8. d.

The Trinity

The doctrine of the Trinity stands as an essential principle of Christian truth. Without this doctrine there is no true Christianity, for the Bible reveals that there is only one God and that He is Father, Son, and Holy Spirit. Jehovah's Witnesses, Mormons, and Christian Science followers all reject the doctrine of the Trinity.[4]

Biblical Christianity affirms one God in three persons. For example, in Isaiah 6:8 God referred to Himself as both singular and plural:

Trinity
God's revelation of Himself as Father, Son, and Holy Spirit, unified in the Godhead yet distinct in person and function

> Who should I send?
> Who will go for Us?
> Isaiah 6:8

In Matthew 28:19 Jesus referred to all three persons of the Trinity: "Go, therefore, and make disciples of all nations, baptizing them in the name of the Father and of the Son and of the Holy Spirit." These persons of the Trinity are not just modes of God's existence or appearance, like three masks worn by an actor. Nor will the Bible allow us to believe in three gods, because as we have seen, it teaches that there is only one God. Yet He is one in three. We must affirm the full deity of the Father, the Son, and the Holy Spirit. Within the perfect fellowship of the Trinity, there is also a perfect order.

Many analogies have been used to illustrate the Trinity and to help in understanding the doctrine. Some have compared the Trinity to a man who, at the same time, is a son, a father, and a grandfather. Others have said it is like the solid, liquid, and vaporous forms of water. However, all analogies ultimately break down.[5] John Dagg wrote about the Trinity: "The Father is God;—the Son is God;—the Holy Ghost is God;—there is but one God."[6] He added that our finite intelligence cannot harmonize the last statement with the preceding three. He wrote, "It is far wiser to admit, that none by searching can find out God; and to abstain from unavailing efforts to comprehend what is incomprehensible to our finite minds."[7] E. Y. Mullins expressed a similar position: "The Bible does not explain the Trinity. It simply gives us the facts ... the briefer the definition of the Trinity, the better for practical purposes. God is revealed to us as Father, Son, and Holy Spirit. These have personal qualities. Yet God is one. This is the New Testament teaching. Beyond this we tend toward speculation."[8]

James T. Draper Jr. wrote, "Perhaps the most challenging truth about God for us to understand is the fact that in the Bible God reveals Himself as Father, Son, and Holy Spirit. Each is a distinct person with specific roles; yet all three have the same essence, nature, and characteristics—they are the same God. God is therefore one God in three persons. Such reality is beyond our ability to comprehend. However, we accept many mysteries in life as true even though we cannot explain them."[9]

When we affirm the Trinity, we stand with Christians throughout all the ages who, like the Apostle Paul, understood the assurance this doctrine brings. As Paul concluded his second letter to the Corinthian church, "The grace of the Lord Jesus Christ, and the love of God, and the fellowship of the Holy Spirit be with all of you" (2 Cor. 13:13).

> Within the perfect fellowship of the Trinity, there is also a perfect order.

Mark each statement _T_ (true) or _F_ (false).

___ 1. There can be no true Christianity without the doctrine of the Trinity.

___ 2. The Bible does not explain the Trinity.

___ 3. God reveals Himself as Father, Son, and Holy Spirit.

___ 4. God is one God in three persons.

___ 5. We cannot fully comprehend the doctrine of the Trinity.

___ 6. The doctrine of the Trinity is not an essential doctrine of our faith.

___ 7. No analogy can adequately illustrate the Trinity.

Which statement best describes the doctrine of the Trinity?

☐ 1. The Trinity is a divine hierarchy: God is first, the Son is second, and the Holy Spirit is third.

☐ 2. God reveals Himself as Father, Son, and Holy Spirit; yet they are the same God.

☐ 3. The Trinity is three separate, divine beings, each distinct from the others.

All of the true/false statements are true except number 6. Statement 2 best describes the Trinity.

Certainties About God

At the foundation of our knowledge of God stand two great truths revealed in the Bible.

Sovereignty
God's unlimited rule of and control over His creation

God's sovereignty. The sovereignty of God is one of the most compromised doctrines in the church. Many who claim to be Christians believe in a God who means well but cannot seem to make His will come to pass, a God who is needy and requires external assistance to accomplish His will, or a God who is not quite sure what He wants done in certain circumstances. This is not the God of the Bible. God is in charge of the universe, and He is guiding it to the time when

the kingdom of the world has become
  the kingdom
of our Lord and of His Messiah,
and He will reign forever and ever!
Revelation 11:15

God's character. God is holy. There is not the slightest imperfection in God, for He is pure and perfect. Isaiah heard the seraphim cry,

Holy, holy, holy is the LORD of Hosts;
His glory fills the whole earth.
Isaiah 6:3

The acknowledgment of God's holiness caused the prophet Isaiah to recognize his sinfulness. In contrast, God does not and cannot sin. He is absolute righteousness, for He is the standard for righteousness and holiness.

Holiness is the quintessential attribute of God's moral character, and it defines all other attributes. God's power is the power of holiness, and His omniscience is a holy knowledge. God's love is a holy love, and His righteousness is a holy righteousness, even as His wrath is a holy and righteous wrath. The doctrine of God's wrath has been banished from far too many pulpits, but God's holiness cannot be understood apart from His determination to punish sin. A holy God demands and deserves a holy people, and thus we are called to be holy as well (see 1 Pet. 1:15-16).

In the end language fails to convey the absolute perfection of God. That's why *The Baptist Faith and Message* summarizes His perfection by explaining that He is "infinite in holiness and all other perfections." This comprehensive affirmation means that in all of His attributes, God is perfect. He possesses all His attributes to an infinite degree, and He is infinitely perfect.

"To conceive of God with respect to any one of His attributes apart from the others is to have only a partial picture of God. He reveals Himself fully in and through Jesus Christ, who is interpreted to us by His Word and through His Holy Spirit."[10]
Herschel Hobbs
1907–95
Pastor, First Baptist Church; Oklahoma City, Oklahoma; president, Southern Baptist Convention, 1961–63

"As the One who called you is holy, you also are to be holy in all your conduct; for it is written, 'Be holy, because I am holy.' "
1 Peter 1:15-16

Review your study about God by reading the following Bible verses. Match each reference with the statement that describes God's nature as set forth in that passage.

___ 1. Deuteronomy 6:4 a. God does not change.
___ 2. Job 37:16 b. God is one.
___ 3. Malachi 3:6 c. God is spirit.
___ 4. 1 Peter 1:15-16 d. God is holy.
___ 5. Genesis 1:1 e. God is our Redeemer.
___ 6. John 4:24 f. God has all knowledge.
___ 7. Psalm 19:14 g. God is the Creator.
___ 8. 1 Peter 5:7 h. God cares about us.

The Scriptures and statements should be matched this way: 1. b, 2. f, 3. a, 4. d, 5. g, 6. c, 7. e, 8. h.

We will learn other truths about God in the next chapter.

What are some ways you can show reverence for God in the following areas of your daily life?

Your home life: _____

Your work: _____

Your social life: _____

Your church life: _____

Your private life: _____

Your use of time: _____

Your use of money: _____

Close your study by using some of the attributes you have studied in this chapter to praise God.

CHAPTER 3

GOD THE FATHER

Article 2A

God the Father

"God as Father reigns with providential care over His universe, His creatures, and the flow of the stream of human history according to the purposes of His grace. He is all powerful, all knowing, all loving, and all wise. God is Father in truth to those who become children of God through faith in Jesus Christ. He is fatherly in His attitude toward all men."[1]

> **Memory Verse**
>
> "Look at the birds of the sky: they don't sow or reap or gather into barns, yet your heavenly Father feeds them. Aren't you worth more than they?" Matthew 6:26

"As a father has compassion on his children, so the LORD has compassion on those who fear Him."
Psalm 103:13

Providence
God's care for and guidance of His creation against all opposition

One of the most amazing truths God reveals about Himself is the fact that He relates to us as Father (see Ps. 103:13). We must never underestimate the power of this relational image. Through His love and care for His creatures, God demonstrates the true character of fatherhood. When Jesus taught us to pray to "our Father, who is in heaven" (Matt. 6:9), He opened our eyes to the fact that God's fatherly love is the foundation of our being and the assurance of our future with Him.

Providential Care

The Bible describes God's love and care for His creation in terms of providence. Literally, *providence* means that God provides for His own, giving us everything we need (see Matt. 6:26). In addition, it means that God is intimately involved in His creation and with His creatures (see Ps. 104). Human beings are the special focus of His concern, and the flow of human history is the account of God's providence.

God makes His providence evident in several ways.

God's providence is seen in His care and protection. God's providential care and the perfection of His creative purpose are demonstrated in the predictable, reliable operation of the natural order. God has made a world in which gravity and other natural laws can be trusted to operate. We are not living in a universe of randomness and blind chance.

The biblical account of Joseph from boyhood in the land of Canaan to old age in the land of Egypt vividly illustrates God's providential care (see Gen. 37–50).

Read Genesis 50:15-21. What did Joseph's brothers plan for him (see v. 20)?

_____

What did God plan for Joseph (see v. 20)?

_____

God's providence is seen in His provision. The miraculous feeding of Elijah when he lived by the Wadi Cherith reminds us that God knows who we are, where we live, and what our needs are.

Read 1 Kings 17:2-7. What did Elijah have for food (see v. 6)?

_____

How did he receive the food (see vv. 4,6)? _____

Just as God saw Elijah's need and provided for him, He knows who you are and cares for you. He knows all about you, and He loves you with an eternal love (see Jer. 31:3).

> God knows all about you, and He loves you with an eternal love.

In the Lord's Prayer Jesus taught us to ask God to "give us today our daily bread" (Matt. 6:9-13). John Broadus (1827–95), another founder of the Southern Baptist Theological Seminary, cautioned that we should not spiritualize this request in verse 11. He wrote, "Bread naturally represents food in general, and all that is necessary to support life, of which bread is commonly esteemed the most important and indispensable part."[2]

Jesus emphasized God's providential care for His children in the Sermon on the Mount.

Read Matthew 6:25-34 and complete the following.
    Jesus instructs us not to _____.
    Verse 25 gives us a lesson from the greater to the lesser:
    • Life is more than _____.
    • The body is more than _____.
    • Because God has given us our lives and our bodies,
       He will surely give us _____.
    Then Jesus gives a lesson from the lesser to the greater
    (see vv. 26-30):
    • God feeds the _____.
    • God clothes the _____.
    • Because God provides for the birds and wildflowers,
       He will surely provide for _____.

God's providence is seen in the moral structure of the universe. God has built into the universe a structure of cause and effect that is evident. For example, sin leads to disaster and judgment. Near the end of his life, Moses presented the Israelites two distinct ways of life. If they obeyed God, they would enjoy God's blessings; if they disobeyed, they would be cursed. Then he admonished them, "Today ... I have set before you life and death, blessing and curse. Choose life so that you and your descendants may live, love the LORD your God, obey Him, and remain faithful to Him" (Deut. 30:19-20). In the New Testament Paul also referred to the consequences that result from moral choices: "Don't be deceived: God is not mocked. For whatever a man sows he will also reap, because the one who sows to his flesh will reap corruption from the flesh, but the one who sows to the Spirit will reap eternal life from the Spirit" (Gal. 6:7-8).

God's providence is seen in the unfolding purpose of God's grace. The record of history is a testimony to God's purpose and providence. In fact, the entire cosmos exists for the supreme purpose of displaying God's glory through the redemption of sinners (see Acts 17:24-31). That incredible fact explains the course of human history and the very meaning of life itself. Of course, only those who know God as Father can understand this truth. To those who do not know God, the very purpose of the universe is beyond understanding.

Define God's providence in your own words.

_____

_____

Name the four ways God's providence is evident in the world.

1. _____

2. _____

3. _____

4. _____

"Having overlooked the times of ignorance, God now commands all people everywhere to repent, because He has set a day on which He is going to judge the world in righteousness by the Man He has appointed. He has provided proof of this to everyone by raising Him from the dead."
Acts 17:30-31

Attributes of God the Father

No language can adequately express the reality of God, but several key words describe important attributes of God—truths about Him that are revealed in the Bible. These are truths we must know and teach.

God is all-powerful. God is omnipotent—His power is not restricted in any way. The Bible describes God as almighty, meaning that He holds all power. In the Old Testament He is revealed as *El Shaddai*—God Almighty (see Gen. 17:1). He is the source of everything, including all power and all powers. No power in heaven or on earth can thwart His plans, frustrate His will, or force His hand. In his vision the Apostle John saw the great multitude of heaven "like the sound of cascading waters, and like the rumbling of loud thunder, saying,

Omnipotent
All-powerful

 Hallelujah—because our Lord God, the Almighty, has begun to reign!
Revelation 19:6

God's omnipotence is a source of comfort and security for His people. No one can defeat or frustrate God's purposes. What He sets out to do, He does. No competing power challenges Him, and no power in heaven or on earth can withstand Him. As King Nebuchadnezzar learned the hard way, "There is no one who can hold back His hand" (Dan. 4:35).

Omnipotent **means that (choose one)—**
☐ God knows all things—past, present, and future;
☐ God is present everywhere;
☐ God is all-powerful;
☐ God loves every person.

Circle the translation of *El Shaddai* in the preceding discussion. How has God been El Shaddai in your life?

_____

_____

Omniscient
All-knowing

"LORD, You have searched me and known me. You know when I sit down and when I stand up; You understand my thoughts from far away. You observe my travels and my rest; You are aware of all my ways. Before a word is on my tongue, You know all about it, LORD."
Psalm 139:1-4

"'I know the plans I have for you'— this is the LORD's declaration—'plans for your welfare, not for disaster, to give you a future and a hope.'"
Jeremiah 29:11

God is all-knowing. God knows all things—past, present, and future. Nothing is hidden from His sight (see Rom. 11:33). God never learns anything, for He has no need of learning. We describe this attribute as His *omniscience.* God's knowledge is all-encompassing and perfect.

As *The Baptist Faith and Message* states, the Bible reveals that God's knowledge "extends to all things, past, present, and future, including the future decisions of His free creatures." Nothing is excluded from His knowledge (see Ps. 50:11). God knows the future perfectly, even our personal decisions. He knows our mind before we know it ourselves (see 1 Kings 8:39; Ps. 142:3). God knows all the people of the earth, and He knows us better than we know ourselves (see Ps. 139:1-4).

Although God is omniscient, human beings are fully responsible for our own decisions and will. Any apparent contradiction on these points results from human confusion and the limits of our understanding. The fact that God knows all things does not mean that He necessarily causes them to happen. God's omniscience does not imply determinism, the belief that God directly causes all events.

God's infinite, comprehensive knowledge also includes foreknowledge. God does not wait to see what will happen. This is comforting to God's people, for we are safe in the care of the One who knows and rules the future. God knows the future perfectly. Herschel Hobbs succinctly stated this truth: "The foreknowledge of God is based upon His omniscience, or all knowledge. Since the Bible views God as present at all times and all places contemporaneously in His universe, He knows all things simultaneously. Thus He foreknows all things before they occur."[3] Does this mean that human beings do not experience moral freedom and bear moral responsibility? Not at all, explained Hobbs: "The Bible does not try to harmonize God's sovereignty and man's free will with respect to His foreknowledge. It assumes them both to be true. This is a mystery to our finite minds but not to the infinite mind of an omniscient God."[4]

Read Jeremiah 29:11 in the margin. What is one way God's foreknowledge can be reassuring and comforting to you?

Omniscient means that (choose one)—

☐ God knows all things—past, present, and future;
☐ God is present everywhere;
☐ God is all-powerful;
☐ God loves every person.

God is all-loving. With breathtaking simplicity the Bible declares that "God is love" (1 John 4:8). God's love is His self-giving nature—His very character as demonstrated through countless acts of compassion and mercy. God's love is not simply a larger and more powerful form of human love. As a matter of fact, human love is a mere reflection of the reality of God's love. Because God's character is perfectly consistent and His love is constant, God's love is our final security. In other words, God's love is matched to His omnipotence, and we can be certain that God's love will never fail (see Ps. 33:5). Unlike human expressions of love, God's love is pure and perfect. No mixed motives, no uncertainties, and no hesitations are present in God's love.

> "The earth is full of the LORD's unfailing love."
> Psalm 33:5

God loves with a redeeming love—a self-giving love. God does not waver in His love for us, nor does He make His love conditional. On the contrary, the Apostle Paul gave us a priceless understanding of God's love when he reminded us, "God proves His own love for us in that while we were still sinners Christ died for us!" (Rom. 5:8). This vital truth is often misconstrued and misrepresented. To present God's love as indulgence or sentimentality is inadequate and inaccurate. God's love is not sentimentality. Instead, it is the costly love of a faithful Father, who shows His love through steadfast character and constancy of judgment. God does not indulge sin or sinners. God is all-loving, but that does not mean He will not punish sin, nor does it mean He will fail to exercise perfect justice. God's love is inextricably tied to His justice and holiness.

What are two ways God's love has been evident in your life this week?

1. _____

2. _____

"Can anyone teach God knowledge, since He judges the exalted ones?"
Job 21:22

"You, Lord, are a compassionate and gracious God, slow to anger and abundant in faithful love and truth."
Psalm 86:15

"Ah, Lord God! You Yourself made the heavens and earth by Your great power and with Your outstretched arm. Nothing is too difficult for You!"
Jeremiah 32:17

"Oh, the depth of the riches both of the wisdom and the knowledge of God! How unsearchable His judgments and untraceable His ways!"
Romans 11:33

God is all-wise. To say that God is all-wise is not the same as saying He is all-knowing, for wisdom exceeds knowledge. The Bible depicts wisdom as the right ordering and understanding of knowledge—the understanding of ultimate meaning and significance. God's wisdom is perfect; He depends on no one for advice or counsel (see Rom. 11:34).

Wisdom is more than understanding. The Bible presents wisdom in a moral context. It is linked not only to accurate knowledge but also to right behavior and right action. God's character and knowledge are perfectly combined and are never separated. This is not true of human beings, who do not always act according to our knowledge. We cannot even understand ourselves completely, as the Apostle Paul made clear: "We know that the law is spiritual; but I am made out of flesh, sold into sin's power. For I do not understand what I am doing, because I do not practice what I want to do, but I do what I hate" (Rom. 7:14-15). In contrast, God always acts in perfect consistency with His perfect character and perfect knowledge. This is what it means to be all-wise.

Humankind's highest privilege is to know God as Father, but as *The Baptist Faith and Message* states, God is truly the Father only "to those who become children of God through faith in Jesus Christ." This vital insight dispels any notion that God is obligated to save all people, without regard to faith in Jesus Christ. At the same time, God "is fatherly in His attitude toward all men." Our task is to tell all people how they can know God as Father by coming to Christ through faith. Then they too will know the infinite love of our faithful Heavenly Father.

Read each Scripture in the margin and match it with the attribute of God to which it refers.

___ 1. Job 21:22	a. Love
___ 2. Psalm 86:15	b. Wisdom
___ 3. Jeremiah 32:17	c. Power
___ 4. Romans 11:33	d. Knowledge

Did you match the verses this way? 1. d, 2. a, 3. c, 4. b and/or d.

Thank God for His love, wisdom, power, and knowledge.

CHAPTER 4

GOD THE SON

Article 2B

God the Son

"Christ is the eternal Son of God. In His incarnation as Jesus Christ He was conceived of the Holy Spirit and born of the virgin Mary. Jesus perfectly revealed and did the will of God, taking upon Himself human nature with its demands and necessities and identifying Himself completely with mankind yet without sin. He honored the divine law by His personal obedience, and in His substitutionary death on the cross He made provision for the redemption of men from sin. He was raised from the dead with a glorified body and appeared to His disciples as the person who was with them before His crucifixion. He ascended into heaven and is now exalted at the right hand of God where He is the One Mediator, fully God, fully man, in whose Person is effected the reconciliation between God and man. He will return in power and glory to judge the world and to consummate His redemptive mission. He now dwells in all believers as the living and ever present Lord."[1]

Memory Verse

"God proves His own love for us in that while we were still sinners Christ died for us!" Romans 5:8

Jesus Christ is the eternal Son of God. This great truth is the first principle of Christianity—the truth on which all other truths are grounded. This single sentence explains the very essence of Christianity, for to know Christ is to know God. John Broadus wrote, "Jesus is the center of the Scriptures. Everything in the Old Testament points forward to Him; everything in the New Testament proceeds forth from Him."[2]

The Eternal Son of God

The full deity and full humanity of Christ are fundamental to true Christianity. The Bible affirms the preexistence of Christ—His existence with the Father before the creation of the world. Just before His crucifixion Jesus prayed to the Father, remembering "that glory I had with You before the world existed" (John 17:5). As with the Father, there never was a time when Christ did not exist—or will not exist.

The Bible also identifies Christ as the agent of creation:

> All things were created through Him,
> and apart from Him not one thing
>   was created
> that has been created.
> John 1:3

In addition, Christ is the Lord over all creation, holding the entire universe together. As the Apostle Paul stated, "He is before all things, and by Him all things hold together" (Col. 1:17). The preeminence of Christ will be revealed to all people one day, but the church knows this truth and understands that this is the very center of our faith.

Read Christ's words in the margin and state how each passage affirms His preexistence.

John 1:1-2: _____

John 8:56: _____

John 8:58: _____

John 10:30: _____

Revelation 22:13: _____

"In the beginning was the Word, and the Word was with God, and the Word was God. He was with God in the beginning."
John 1:1-2

"Your father Abraham was overjoyed that he would see My day; he saw it and rejoiced."
John 8:56

"Before Abraham was, I am."
John 8:58

"The Father and I are one."
John 10:30

"I am the Alpha and the Omega, the First and the Last, the Beginning and the End."
Revelation 22:13

The Birth of Christ

God's coming to earth in human flesh is the greatest event in human history; yet it was largely hidden from the world's view—at least at first. Not only is the story of Jesus' humble birth in Bethlehem the essence of the Christmas story, but it also signals the beginning of Christ's earthly ministry. Speaking to shepherds, the angel declared that the baby was "a Savior, who is Christ the Lord" (Luke 2:11, NASB). The angel told the shepherds that this baby was the promised Savior, the Messiah and Lord over all. What a declaration!

Christ's coming in human form is called the incarnation; He was literally God in human flesh. As John put it, the eternal Word "became flesh and took up residence among us" (John 1:14). This was an act of infinite humility, as Christ

> emptied Himself by assuming the form
>   of a slave,
> taking on the likeness of men.
> Philippians 2:7

Incarnation
The divine Son Jesus' coming to and living on earth in human form

He who made the universe came into His own creation to save His people. This is the distinctive truth of the Christian faith: in Jesus, God came and dwelled among us.

Incarnation **means that (choose one)—**
- ☐ Jesus Christ is God;
- ☐ Jesus Christ came to earth in human form;
- ☐ Jesus Christ exemplified infinite humility;
- ☐ Jesus Christ died for our sins.

In the incarnation Christ came to earth in human form. His birth was no ordinary birth. In the first place, He was conceived by the Holy Spirit and was born to the virgin Mary. The doctrine of the virgin birth is essential to Christianity, for it is central to understanding who Jesus is. He came in true human flesh, though He was not conceived by a human father. This is a miracle that is beyond our full understanding, but it affirms the supernatural nature of Christ's birth and

41

the fact that He was conceived without sin. Thus, He can identify with us in our humanity without the stain of sin.

The fact of Christ's virgin birth should not be hard to accept. As the angel Gabriel reassured young Mary when she first heard that she would give birth to the Son of God, "Nothing will be impossible with God" (Luke 1:37). John Dagg wrote, "The divine power, which formed a man out of the dust of the ground, could also form a man in the womb of the virgin."[3] James Draper wrote, "Jesus' unique virgin birth revealed His supernatural nature as the Son of God. In Jesus, God came to earth in the flesh. Therefore, unlike any other human, Jesus lived without sin as perfect humanity and perfect divinity."[4]

The Life of Christ

Jesus lived as the Son of Man and the Son of God, both in one, fully human, fully divine. R. G. Lee contrasted Jesus' humanity and deity:

> As a man, He got tired; as God, He said, "Come unto me, all ye that labour and are heavy laden, and I will give you rest."
>
> As man, He got hungry; as God, he fed thousands with a lad's lunch.
>
> As man, He got thirsty; as God, He gave living water.
>
> As a man, He prayed; as God, he made, in praying, no confession of sin.
>
> As man, He was tempted in all points like as we are; as God, He was without sin, baffling his enemies with the question, "Who convinceth me of sin?"
>
> As man, He slept; as God, He arose from sleep and stilled the raging tempest. ...
>
> As man, a ship carried Him; as God, He walked on the rolling, tumbling sea.
>
> As man, He accepted a village girl's invitation to her wedding; as God, He there changed water into wine. ...
>
> As man, He wept at Lazarus' grave; as God, He raised Lazarus from the dead.[6]

"If Jesus was not virgin born, we have no Saviour, no integrity, no credibility, no authority, no reliability of the Scriptures. All these are involved in the truth of the virgin birth. If Christ was born of man and not of God, Calvary has no meaning— the Gospels are not good news but issues of falsehood. The resurrection is unthinkable without the supernatural birth."[5]

R. G. Lee
1886–1978
Pastor, Bellevue Baptist Church; Memphis, Tennessee; president, Southern Baptist Convention, 1949–51

Jesus' earthly ministry fulfilled a prophecy of Isaiah that Jesus read in the synagogue at Nazareth one Sabbath day:

> The Spirit of the Lord God is on Me,
> because the LORD has anointed Me
> to bring good news to the poor.
> He has sent Me to heal the brokenhearted,
> to proclaim liberty to the captives,
> and freedom to the prisoners;
> to proclaim the year of the LORD's favor.
> Isaiah 61:1-2

In His perfect humanity Christ perfectly identified with us; yet He did not sin. His life was marked by perfect obedience—the very obedience that was expected of Adam and Eve in the garden of Eden. Unlike our first parents, Jesus never sinned. Nevertheless, He fully identified with us in our sin—and even in our temptation—for He "has been tested in every way as we are, yet without sin" (Heb. 4:15). As the Book of Hebrews explains, this fact should give us great encouragement to "approach the throne of grace with boldness, so that we may receive mercy and find grace to help us at the proper time" (Heb. 4:16). Christ fulfilled all of the righteous requirements of the law—something no other person could ever do. His perfect obedience was evident at every moment of His life and took Him to His death.

In His perfect humanity Christ perfectly identified with us; yet He did not sin.

Review the previous section. Underline three evidences of Jesus' humanity. Circle three evidences of Jesus' deity.

The Death of Christ

Jesus came to die. John the Baptist declared this when he first met Jesus, telling his disciples, "Here is the Lamb of God, who takes away the sin of the world!" (John 1:29). At first even Jesus' own disciples did not understand that He must die. Just after Peter correctly acknowledged Him as "the Messiah, the Son of the living God" (Matt. 16:16), Jesus told His followers that He must "suffer many things from the elders, chief priests, and scribes, be killed, and

"According to the law almost everything is purified with blood, and without the shedding of blood there is no forgiveness."
Hebrews 9:22

"You were redeemed from your empty way of life inherited from the fathers, not with perishable things, like silver or gold, but with the precious blood of Christ, like that of a lamb without defect or blemish."
1 Peter 1:18-19

"In Him we have redemption through His blood, the forgiveness of our trespasses, according to the riches of His grace."
Ephesians 1:7

be raised the third day" (Matt. 16:21). His death was not an unfortunate thing that happened to Him but was the Father's plan from the beginning. As Peter declared in his great sermon on the day of Pentecost, Christ "was delivered up according to God's determined plan and foreknowledge" (Acts 2:23).

Why did Jesus have to die? The answer to that question reaches to the depth of our human sinfulness and to the infinite glory of God's holiness. God is not only a God of love but also the Holy One who cannot allow sin to go unpunished. Jesus died for sinners. No one took His life from Him, for the Good Shepherd "lays down His life for His sheep" (John 10:11). His death was the perfect sacrifice for our sins—the only sacrifice acceptable to the Father.

Read Hebrews 9:22 in the margin. The basis of the forgiveness of sins is _____.

Read 1 Peter 1:18-19 and Ephesians 1:7 in the margin. The basis of our redemption and forgiveness is

_____.

God had long ago told His people that a blood sacrifice was required for the forgiveness of sin. As He spoke through Moses, God instructed the Israelites that "the life of a creature is in the blood, and I have appointed it to you to make atonement on the altar for your lives, since it is the lifeblood that makes atonement" (Lev. 17:11). The Book of Hebrews further explains, "Without the shedding of blood there is no forgiveness" (Heb. 9:22).

How did Christ's death result in the salvation of sinners? Paul explained, "God presented Him as a propitiation through faith in His blood, to demonstrate His righteousness" (Rom. 3:25). The concept of propitiation is often misunderstood. Forgiveness and the covering of sins are certainly part of the concept, but the biblical meaning relates primarily to God's wrath. The Criswell Study Bible explains the meaning of propitiation: "God's wrath is a settled disposition against evil. The just demands of God's holiness for the punishment and exclusion of sin must be satisfied. Propitiation is the work of Christ on the cross in which He met the demands of the righteousness of God against sin, both satisfying the requirements of God's justice and canceling the guilt of man."[7] Paul further emphasized that Christ's death simultaneously showed God's mercy and righteousness, "so that He would be righteous and declare righteous the one who has faith in Jesus" (Rom. 3:26). This is an astounding explanation. God's righteousness required that He demand a perfect sacrifice in blood, but God's love and mercy led Him to provide that sacrifice in the person of His own Son. Having met the requirements of His own righteousness and of His redeeming love, the Father is publicly shown to be both just and the justifier of those who come to Christ by faith.

Underline the definition of *propitiation* above.

To speak of Christ's substitutionary death is to affirm what the Bible so clearly teaches—that Christ died in our place. As Paul told the Romans, "Christ died for the ungodly" (Rom. 5:6). This act was the supreme demonstration of God's love: "God proves His love for us in that while we were still sinners Christ died for us" (Rom. 5:8).

John Broadus stated, "By far the most wonderful thing that has ever happened in the universe, is the atoning death of Jesus Christ the Lord.[8] ... Christ took our place and died like a sinner, that we might take His place and be righteous in Him."[9] Paul wrote, "He made the One who did not know sin to be sin for us, so that we might become the righteousness of God in Him" (2 Cor. 5:21). R. G. Lee explained, "All our guilt was charged to Christ's account. By His crucifixion, He has discharged all our liabilities. So now, being *in* Christ, we have no account to discharge. In God's sight, we are as righteous as He—and *in* Him we are accepted."[10]

The substitutionary death of Christ means that (choose one)—

- ☐ Christ died as our example;
- ☐ Christ died as a substitute for works;
- ☐ Christ died in our place;
- ☐ Christ died to replace the law.

Atonement
God's overcoming sin through Christ's obedience and death to restore believers to a right relationship with God

Propitiation
Jesus' work on the cross to satisfy God's righteous demand against sin

Substitutionary
Jesus died in our place, paying the price for our sin.

"In the cross, the believer finds the strongest motive to holiness. As we stand before it, and view the exhibition of the Saviour's love, we resolve to live to Him who died for us. The world ceases to charm. … Sin appears infinitely hateful. We regard it as the accursed thing which caused the death of our beloved Lord. … The cross is a holy place, where we learn to be like Christ … and to delight in the law of God which was in His heart. In the presence of the cross, we feel that omnipotent grace has hold of our heart; and we surrender to dying love."[11]

John Dagg
1794–1884
Baptist pastor, teacher, and administrator

Christ's substitutionary death means that He died in our place. In accomplishing this perfect sacrifice, Christ fulfilled and completed what had begun under the old covenant, when the priests had sacrificed animals to atone for the sins of the people. As the Book of Hebrews makes clear, those animal sacrifices were limited and temporary. Under the Old Testament system the priests had to enter the holy of holies each year to make atonement. Through His death on the cross, Christ "entered the holy of holies once for all, not by the blood of goats and calves, but by His own blood, having obtained eternal redemption" (Heb. 9:12). Thus, Christ is "the mediator of a new covenant" (Heb. 9:15), the "one mediator between God and man" (1 Tim. 2:5).

The focus of Christ's redeeming work is the cross, an ancient instrument of execution. On the cross Jesus gave His life for sinners, suffering and dying in our place. When we sing of the cross, we point back to God's act that accomplished our salvation. Paul told the Galatians that he would boast only in the cross of Jesus Christ, "through whom the world has been crucified to me, and I to the world" (Gal. 6:14). To the unbelieving world, the cross is foolishness, but to those who are being saved, it is the power of God (see 1 Cor. 1:18).

Pause and thank God for what Christ did on the cross.

The Resurrection and Ascension of Christ

God's power raised Jesus from the dead. The resurrection of Christ is the basis of our hope and the proof of Christ's victory over sin and death. Without the resurrection Jesus Christ is merely the victim of a human conspiracy that ended on the cross. Raised from the dead, Christ is revealed as both Savior and Lord. Christ's resurrection is absolutely essential to the Christian faith. Without the resurrection there is no Christianity. The Apostle Paul powerfully made this point when he taught the Corinthian Christians that "if Christ has not been raised, then our preaching is without foundation, and so is your faith" (1 Cor. 15:14). Furthermore, "if Christ has not been raised, your faith is worthless; you are still in your sins" (1 Cor. 15:17).

But Christ has been raised from the dead. His resurrection was an event in space and time, the literal resurrection of His body. After the resurrection Thomas was able to place his hand in the Savior's wounded side and declare, "My Lord and My God!" (John 20:28). Christ's resurrected body was fully alive, characterized by real flesh. At the same time, the resurrection body is different from the perishable bodies we now possess. Christians are promised that one day when we are raised with Christ, we will be given resurrection bodies. Paul explained that "flesh and blood cannot inherit the kingdom of God, and corruption cannot inherit incorruption" (1 Cor. 15:50). But through the resurrection power of the Lord Jesus Christ, believers will also be raised from the dead, given resurrection bodies, and "clothed with immortality" (1 Cor. 15:53). To the Romans Paul put it this way: "If the Spirit of Him who raised Jesus from the dead lives in you, then He who raised Christ from the dead will also bring your mortal bodies to life through His spirit who lives in you" (Rom. 8:11).

John Broadus explained that the resurrection validates the Christian faith: "The resurrection of the Lord Jesus establishes the truth of Christianity. The apostle Paul says He is declared to be the Son of God by the resurrection from the dead. ... It declared Him to be all that He had ever professed to be, and so it establishes the truth of all His teachings and the truth of the whole Christian society. The great fact that Jesus Christ rose from the dead is the central fact of the evidence of Christianity."[12]

The resurrection was central to the faith of the apostles and to their preaching. On the day of Pentecost, Peter proclaimed that God had raised Jesus Christ, "ending the pains of death, because it was not possible for Him to be held by it" (Acts 2:24). Standing before the Sanhedrin, Peter and John testified of Christ's resurrection, identifying themselves as followers of "Jesus Christ the Nazarene—whom you crucified and whom God raised from the dead" (Acts 4:10). The resurrection is affirmed in all four Gospels and confirmed throughout the New Testament. The risen Christ was seen by hundreds of observers and was recognized by His followers (see 1 Cor. 15:1-8). The resurrection gave the early Christians confidence to face hardship, death, and martyrdom. Just as the resurrection was central to the faith of the earliest Christians, it must be central to our faith as well.

"A man has to discredit all testimony and has to discard all the laws of evidence if he repudiates or calls in question the great teaching of the resurrection of Jesus from the grave. ... A fact as thoroughly authenticated as any fact in all history is the fact that Jesus of Nazareth, crucified under Pontius Pilate, and buried in Joseph's new tomb, on the third day came out of the grave, a triumphant man, a triumphant God, over the power of death."[13]

George W. Truett
1867–1944
Pastor, First Baptist Church; Dallas, Texas; president, Southern Baptist Convention, 1927–29

Broadus identified the practical significance of the resurrection: "The resurrection of Christ is not only a pillar of Christian evidence, but has important theological and practical relations. (a) It completed His work of atonement, and stamped it with divine approval. ... (b) It is the ground and pledge of His people's resurrection. ... Of their spiritual resurrection, to walk in newness of life. ... Of the resurrection of the body. ... (c) It is represented in baptism. ... (d) It is celebrated on the Lord's Day."[14]

Just weeks after the resurrection, Christ ascended to the Father. Christ was blessing His disciples when "He left them and was carried up into heaven" (Luke 24:51). A cloud received Jesus out of their sight. As the disciples watched, two men in white clothes appeared to them. "They said, 'Men of Galilee, why do you stand looking up into heaven? This Jesus, who has been taken from you into heaven, will come in the same way that you have seen Him going into heaven' " (Acts 1:11).

Write the way you would respond to a neighbor who asked you, "Why do you believe in the resurrection of Christ?"

_____

_____

_____

_____

_____

"The whole Bible has been capsuled in the summary: Jesus is coming; Jesus has come; Jesus is coming again. The return of the Lord is the great hope of the people of God, and it will be the consummation of all things."[15]

Jerry Vines
1937–
Pastor emeritus, First Baptist Church; Jacksonville, Florida; president, Southern Baptist Convention, 1988–90

The Return of Christ

Christ's ascension connects His earthly ministry with His return. The return of Jesus Christ is referred to more than 380 times in the New Testament.[16] The Bible clearly reveals that Christ is coming again—this time in power and in glory. When He returns, He will claim His church, complete His mission, bring all things to consummation, judge the world, and be revealed as the Lord of all creation. Christ's return will be bodily, visible, glorious, and triumphant. Christians look to Christ's return with anticipation and hope, knowing God's purposes will be accomplished and Christ will claim His church and vindicate His people.

Even as the church looks to Christ's return in anticipation and confident hope, we are assured that He is even now the Lord of His church. Christ dwells within the hearts of His people. Seated at the right hand of the Father, Christ intercedes for us (see Rom. 8:34). He is the Mediator, and His ministry of intercession is vital for the security and safety of His people. We are safe in His care, and nothing can separate us from the love of Christ (see Rom. 8:35).

Baptists have been faithful through the centuries in defending the biblical teachings about Jesus Christ. E. Y. Mullins, both in guiding the writing of the first official Southern Baptist statement of faith, *The Baptist Faith and Message,* in 1925 and in his own writings, clearly set forth the biblical truths about Christ: "Jesus Christ was born of the virgin Mary through the power of the Holy Spirit. He was the divine and eternal Son of God. He wrought miracles, healing the sick, casting out demons, raising the dead. He died as the vicarious atoning Savior of the world and was buried. He arose again from the dead. The tomb was emptied of its contents. In his risen body He appeared many times to His disciples. He ascended to the right hand of the Father. He will come again in person, the same Jesus who ascended from the Mount of Olives."[17]

Heretics and false teachers have always directed their attacks on the doctrines most closely connected with Jesus Christ. The believing church must always confront these false teachings and doctrinal errors with vigor and truth (see Gal. 1:6-9). We must be ready to defend the virgin birth of Christ, His full deity, His full humanity, His miraculous acts, His bodily resurrection, His victorious return, and the substitutionary character of His atonement—as well as all the other biblical truths about Jesus Christ. Compromise on these doctrines will be fatal to our witness and subversive of our faith. We stand on the solid rock as we declare these great doctrines of Christian faith. Faithfulness to Christ demands that we cling to Him and serve Him all our days.

> "Christ Jesus is the One who died, but even more, has been raised; He also is at the right hand of God and intercedes for us. Who can separate us from the love of Christ? Can affliction or anguish or persecution or famine or nakedness or danger or sword?"
> Romans 8:34-35

Read *The Baptist Faith and Message* article on God the Son, page 39, and answer the following questions.

In what manner was Jesus' birth supernatural? _____

_____

How did Jesus identify with humankind? _____

_____

How did Jesus honor divine law? _____

_____

How did Jesus make provision for redemption?

_____

How did Jesus appear to His disciples after
His resurrection? _____

_____

Where is Jesus now? _____

_____

What is Jesus' present position? _____

_____

How will Jesus return to earth? _____

_____

Why will Jesus return to earth? _____

_____

What is Jesus' present relationship to believers? _____

_____

Thank God for Christ's preexistence, birth, life, death on the cross, resurrection, ascension, and promised return.

CHAPTER 5

GOD THE HOLY SPIRIT

Red flag
when a pastor
says God revealed
Something to
them.

Article 2C

God the Holy Spirit

"The Holy Spirit is the Spirit of God, fully divine. He inspired holy men of old to write the Scriptures. Through illumination He enables men to understand truth. He exalts Christ. He convicts men of sin, of righteousness, and of judgment. He calls men to the Saviour, and effects regeneration. At the moment of regeneration He baptizes every believer into the Body of Christ. He cultivates Christian character, comforts believers, and bestows the spiritual gifts by which they serve God through His church. He seals the believer unto the day of final redemption. His presence in the Christian is the guarantee that God will bring the believer into the fullness of the stature of Christ. He enlightens and empowers the believer and the church in worship, evangelism, and service."[1]

Memory Verse

"Don't get drunk with wine, which leads to reckless actions, but be filled with the Spirit." Ephesians 5:18

Many Christians know very little about the Holy Spirit. This is a great tragedy, for the Holy Spirit is fully divine and perfectly does the Father's will. Throughout the Bible the Holy Spirit is identified as the divine agent behind many of the most important events in God's dealings with humankind. The Spirit has a role in many aspects of our salvation. As the spiritual manifestation of God, the Holy Spirit is at work among us even now, just as He has been at work since before the creation of the world.

The Baptist Faith and Message begins this article by stating that the Holy Spirit "is the Spirit of God, fully divine." This reminds us to keep the doctrine of the Trinity in the forefront of our understanding. The Holy Spirit is a person, not an inanimate or depersonalized force. As the Spirit of God and the Spirit of Christ, He is of the same nature as the Father and the Son. W. A. Criswell wrote, "The Holy Spirit is God. He has all the attributes of God. He is eternal, according to Hebrews 9; He is omnipotent, according to Genesis 1; He is omniscient, according to 1 Corinthians 2; He is omnipresent, according to Psalm 139."[2]

The Holy Spirit Inspired God's Word

Scripture reveals that the Holy Spirit played a vital role in the creation of God's written Word. *The Baptist Faith and Message* states that the Holy Spirit inspired "holy men of old to write the Scriptures." The written Word of God is one of God's greatest gifts to us. The inspiration of the Holy Spirit explains how the Bible can simultaneously be the words of men and the Word of God.

Peter tells us that "moved by the Holy Spirit, men spoke from God" (2 Pet. 1:21). This verse confirms the Bible's inspiration, but it does not imply dictation. The Holy Spirit did not place these writers in a trance or rob them of their creative abilities. On the contrary, the Bible presents the process of inspiration—verbal plenary inspiration—as the Holy Spirit moving the human authors of Scripture to write exactly what He wanted them to write. At the same time, the words the human authors wrote were the very words they wanted to write. This is because the Holy Spirit works within believers to accomplish His sovereign purposes. Thus, Paul taught Timothy to honor the Bible as the fully inspired Word of God (see 2 Tim. 3:16-17).

The Holy Spirit works within believers to accomplish His sovereign purposes.

The Holy Spirit Ministers to People

The Holy Spirit is responsible for a number of ministries to bring people to belief in Christ and to nurture believers' spiritual lives.

The Holy Spirit convicts of sin. The Holy Spirit convicts "the world about sin, righteousness, and judgment" (John 16:8). Without the work of the Holy Spirit, we would not see sin for what it is, and we would be blind to the reality of our unrighteousness. Furthermore, we would be ignorant or unconcerned about the judgment that is to come.

> Without the work of the Holy Spirit, we would not see sin for what it is.

How did you come to realize your lostness and your need for a Savior?

How did the Holy Spirit convict you of sin?

The Holy Spirit calls unbelievers to salvation. God's work of salvation includes the special ministry of the Holy Spirit. The Holy Spirit, having convicted the sinner of sin, also calls the sinner to Christ. As the Book of Revelation presents the gospel call, "Both the Spirit and the bride say, 'Come!' Anyone who hears should say, 'Come!' And the one who is thirsty should come. Whoever desires should take the living water as a gift" (Rev. 22:17). God calls sinners to Christ through the internal witness of the Holy Spirit, even as God uses the external witness of the Bible and the gospel presentation.

The Holy Spirit brings regeneration. Regeneration is also the Holy Spirit's work. When Peter preached at Caesarea, "the Holy Spirit came down on all those who heard the message" (Acts 10:44). And as Jesus told Nicodemus, "Whatever is born of the flesh is flesh, and whatever is born of the Spirit is spirit" (John 3:6). Jesus' words picture the Holy Spirit's role in effecting regeneration—the new birth—as He calls us to faith in Christ.

The Holy Spirit indwells believers. Some churches teach that Christians should look for a second blessing, described as a baptism of the Holy Spirit, that is separate from the gift of the Spirit at the moment of regeneration. *The Baptist Faith and Message* clearly excludes this teaching. Baptists believe that the gift of the Spirit comes when, "at the moment of regeneration He baptizes every believer into the Body of Christ." As Peter proclaimed the gospel on the day of Pentecost, "Repent ... and be baptized, each of you, in the name of Jesus the Messiah for the forgiveness of your sins, and you will receive the gift of the Holy Spirit" (Acts 2:38).

The Holy Spirit seals believers. The Holy Spirit seals the believer's salvation and serves as the absolute assurance that God's saving work will be completed in the believer's life. In the Holy Spirit believers are sealed "for the day of redemption" and thus abide in Christ (Eph. 4:30; also see 1 John 4:13).

> "Don't grieve God's Holy Spirit, who sealed you for the day of redemption."
> Ephesians 4:30

> "This is how we know that we remain in Him and He in us: He has given to us from His Spirit."
> 1 John 4:13

The Holy Spirit illuminates truth. The Holy Spirit illuminates believers' spiritual discernment so that they understand truth. As Paul wrote to the Corinthians, "We have not received the spirit of the world, but the Spirit who is from God, in order to know what has been freely given to us by God. We also speak these things, not in words taught by human wisdom, but in those taught by the Spirit, explaining spiritual things to spiritual people" (1 Cor. 2:12-13).

Criswell identified the enlightening work of the Holy Spirit with the presence of Jesus Himself: "Jesus is no longer with us in the flesh to explain to us all of the things that we need to know and to show us all the things that we need to do. The Holy Spirit is given to us that we might have the wisdom, the direction, and the illumination the living presence of our Lord would otherwise provide. ... He takes the place of Jesus in the flesh. Jesus has returned to heaven and the Spirit of Jesus, which is Jesus Himself, is here with us. In practical religion it is impossible to distinguish between the Spirit of Christ in the heart and Christ Himself in the heart. ... When we possess the Holy Spirit, we possess Jesus."[3]

The Holy Spirit teaches believers. The Holy Spirit works within believers to produce an understanding of spiritual things. This is one of the Holy Spirit's most important works in believers. He opens our eyes so that we can understand the Scriptures, the gospel, and the deep truths of God. The Holy Spirit also exalts Christ. "He will glorify Me," Christ said, "because He will take from what is Mine and declare it to you" (John 16:14). In other words, the Holy Spirit is our constant Teacher, opening our understanding to the things of God and applying these truths to our lives. In doing so, the Holy Spirit exalts Christ and brings glory to God through the maturation of Christ's people: "When the Spirit of truth comes, He will guide you into all the truth. For He will not speak on His own, but He will speak whatever He hears. He will also declare to you what is to come" (John 16:13).

> The Holy Spirit works within believers to produce an understanding of spiritual things.

Reflect on your life. Identify two ways the Holy Spirit has guided you.

1. _____

2. _____

Jesus prepared His disciples for His death, resurrection, and ascension by promising them, "I will ask the Father, and He will give you another Counselor to be with you forever. He is the Spirit of truth. The world is unable to receive Him because it doesn't see Him or know Him. But you do know Him, because He remains with you and will be in you" (John 14:16-17). The promised helper is the Holy Spirit. Jesus told His disciples that the Holy Spirit "will teach you all things and remind you of everything I have told you" (John 14:26).

The Holy Spirit intercedes for believers. During our earthly service to God, the Holy Spirit intercedes for believers "with groanings too deep for words," pleading for us in ways we do not even know to ask (Rom. 8:26, NASB). This is one of the sweetest and most crucial works of the Holy Spirit in the lives of God's redeemed people.

Mark each statement *T* (true) or *F* (false).

____ 1. The Holy Spirit is a force, not a person.

____ 2. The Holy Spirit overrode the personalities of the writers of Scripture.

____ 3. The Holy Spirit lives in every believer.

____ 4. The Holy Spirit indwells believers from the moment of salvation.

____ 5. The Holy Spirit baptizes believers into the body of Christ at the moment of salvation.

____ 6. The baptism of the Spirit is an experience that comes to some believers after conversion.

____ 7. The Holy Spirit seals believers for the day of redemption.

Statements 1, 2, and 6 are false; 3, 4, 5, and 7 are true.

The Holy Spirit Builds the Church

The Holy Spirit works not only within a believer's life but also within the church, for the church of the Lord Jesus Christ is a church made alive in the Spirit. *The Baptist Faith and Message* states that the Holy Spirit "cultivates Christian character, comforts believers, and bestows the spiritual gifts by which they serve God through His church." Believers are not to "walk according to the flesh but according to the Spirit," setting their minds on the things of God (Rom. 8:4).

> Unity is one of the Holy Spirit's greatest gifts to the church.

The Holy Spirit brings unity. Unity is one of the Holy Spirit's greatest gifts to the church. Paul reminded the Corinthians, "We were all baptized by one Spirit into one body—whether Jews or Greeks, whether slaves or free—and we were all made to drink of one Spirit" (1 Cor. 12:13). Paul also instructed the Ephesians to be diligent to keep "the unity of the Spirit with the peace that binds us" (Eph. 4:3). "There is one body and one Spirit," Paul explained, "just as you were called to one hope at your calling; one Lord, one faith, one baptism, one God and Father of all, who is above all and through all and in all" (Eph. 4:4-6).

The Holy Spirit bestows spiritual gifts. The Holy Spirit gives gifts to believers as part of the church: "There are different gifts," Paul asserted, "but the same Spirit" (1 Cor. 12:4). The Spirit distributes gifts to all Christians (see 1 Pet. 4:10), building the body of Christ through the variety of gifts that strengthen the church as a body, "but one and the same Spirit is active in all these, distributing to each one as He wills" (1 Cor. 12:11).

The church is strengthened as the Spirit distributes spiritual gifts to each member, knowing exactly what the church needs and how God's people will best be strengthened by these gifts. Paul warned Christians not to be envious of others' gifts but to exercise the gift God has given. Every believer is given at least one gift as God sovereignly wills, but no one gift is given to all believers.

Spiritual Gift
A God-given ability to serve Christ through His church

"As each one has received a special gift, employ it in serving one another, as good stewards of the manifold grace of God."
1 Peter 4:10, NASB

Read Romans 12:3-8 and 1 Corinthians 12:1-11. As you read, pause and think about each gift bestowed by the Holy Spirit. Complete the following statements.

The main gift the Holy Spirit has given me is

_____.

I am using this gift in the body of Christ by

_____.

Read each Scripture and match the reference with the ministry of the Holy Spirit to which it refers.

____ 1. Ephesians 1:13-14   a. Inspired Scripture
____ 2. Revelation 22:17   b. Teaches, guides
____ 3. Ephesians 4:7-8   c. Convicts of sin
____ 4. John 16:7-11   d. Invites to Christ
____ 5. 2 Peter 1:21   e. Regenerates
____ 6. Titus 3:5-6   f. Dwells in believers
____ 7. 1 Corinthians 2:13   g. Bestows gifts
____ 8. 1 Corinthians 3:16   h. Seals believers

The answers are 1. h, 2. d, 3. g, 4. c, 5. a, 6. e, 7. b, 8. f.

Write one new thing you have learned about the Holy Spirit in your study of this chapter.

_____

_____

Rate the degree to which you are aware of the Holy Spirit's presence in your life.

	Not much			Very much	
While alone	1	2	3	4	5
While at work	1	2	3	4	5
While with my family	1	2	3	4	5
While at church	1	2	3	4	5
When serving the Lord	1	2	3	4	5
In my personal devotions	1	2	3	4	5
In my social life	1	2	3	4	5
In my recreation	1	2	3	4	5

What is one action you can take to live more fully under the Holy Spirit's guidance?

_____

Close your study of this chapter by praying aloud the following hymn.

Holy Spirit, breathe on me,
Until my heart is clean;
Let sunshine fill its inmost part,
With not a cloud between.

Holy Spirit, breathe on me,
Till I am all Thine own,
Until my will is lost in Thine,
To live for Thee alone.[4]

CHAPTER 6

MAN

Article 3
Man

"Man is the special creation of God, made in His own image. He created them male and female as the crowning work of His creation. The gift of gender is thus part of the goodness of God's creation. In the beginning man was innocent of sin and was endowed by his Creator with freedom of choice. By his free choice man sinned against God and brought sin into the human race. Through the temptation of Satan man transgressed the command of God, and fell from his original innocence whereby his posterity inherit a nature and an environment inclined toward sin. Therefore, as soon as they are capable of moral action, they become transgressors and are under condemnation. Only the grace of God can bring man into His holy fellowship and enable man to fulfill the creative purpose of God. The sacredness of human personality is evident in that God created man in His own image, and in that Christ died for man; therefore, every person of every race possesses full dignity and is worthy of respect and Christian love."[1]

Memory Verse

"God created man in His own image;

He created him in the image of God;

He created them male and female." Genesis 1:27

The creation of human beings represents God's crowning act in creation. According to Genesis 2:7, God "formed man of dust from the ground, and breathed into his nostrils the breath of life; and man became a living being." The biblical view of humanity sets the Christian worldview in direct opposition to current ideologies, such as secular humanism and evolution. When the ancient Greek philosopher Protagoras declared that humans are the measure of all things, he articulated the motto of what we know today as the philosophy of humanism. But the Bible says we are not the measure of all things, for we are not even able to understand ourselves without God's revelation. Instead, we should ask with the psalmist, "What is man, that You are mindful of him?" (Ps. 8:4). Our frame of reference must never begin with human beings.

The theory of evolution argues that human beings, along with all other living creatures, are simply the products of a blind, naturalistic process of evolutionary development. Thus, humans are distinct from other animals only in terms of brain size or other capacities. By definition evolution has no room for the concept that humans are made in the image of God, for evolutionary theory has no room for God. The Bible affirms that humans are not accidents or mere animals living among other animals. Human beings alone are made in God's image.

Made in God's Image

As the Bible makes clear, human beings—both male and female—were created in God's image (see Gen. 1:27; 2:7; Col. 3:10). Of course, this does not mean we look like God, for God is spirit. It means we possess a spiritual capacity that makes us moral creatures who can know and worship God (see Deut. 10:12; Ps. 29:2; 42:1; 139:1). Though all creation declares the glory of God, only humans have a moral consciousness (see Rom. 2:15; 1 Cor. 8:7) and the ability to know God. By making us in His image, God sets humanity apart from the rest of creation, and His purpose of redemption is directed specifically to the salvation of sinful humanity. Our creation in God's image explains why we were made for work, action, communication, and reflection.

Image of God
Human beings' spiritual capacity and the ability to fellowship with God

Human beings are the only self-conscious creatures. A dog may dig a hole, but it never sits back to ponder the meaning of the hole. Birds fly through the air, but they have no idea why God made them to do so. Fish swim across oceans, but they never write books about the experience. The entire animal kingdom declares the glory of God, but the animals are unaware of this great fact. Human beings, as the only creatures made in God's image, are made to know God.

Image of God in human beings refers to (choose one)—
☐ our intellectual and reasoning ability;
☐ our dominion over all creation;
☐ our spiritual capacity—ability to fellowship with God;
☐ our physical appearance and ability to walk upright.

Image of God refers to our spiritual capacity and ability to fellowship with God. God made us as spiritual beings, so we have an innate desire for fellowship with Him. We possess a soul, described in the Bible as our spiritual capacity and inner knowledge. The soul is eternal, surviving death. At the same time, we are also embodied creatures. The body is a gift from God and is the temple of the Holy Spirit, who dwells in us. We are to take care of our bodies out of respect for God, but Christians must not worship the body. Our bodily needs, desires, pleasures, and pains remind us of our constant dependence on God and of God's glory and power that He wants to reveal in us (see 2 Cor. 12:7-10).

Mark each statement *T* (true) or *F* (false).
____ 1. Humans are both physical and spiritual beings.
____ 2. Our bodily needs remind us of our constant dependence on God.
____ 3. The soul is the inner inclination toward sin.
____ 4. People have an innate hunger for God.
____ 5. We should give top priority to the body.
____ 6. Spirituality means renouncing physical pleasures.
____ 7. The conscience and the soul are identical.
____ 8. We should care for the body but not worship it.
____ 9. The soul is our spiritual capacity and inner knowledge.

Statements 1, 2, 4, 8, and 9 are true; 3, 5, 6, and 7 are false.

"There is something in man that will not be satisfied with the seen and the temporal. Something in him cries out for the spiritual and the eternal. Man thirsts for God. In the midst of the visible and the transient, he reaches out after the invisible and the abiding. The Psalmist voices this universal cry of the human heart when he says: 'As the hart panteth after the water brooks, so panteth my soul after thee, O God' (Psalm 42:1). Wherever men have been found they have had some form of religion. ... All men of all races and climes have cried out for God."[2]

W. T. Conner
1877–1952
Professor, Southwestern Baptist Theological Seminary

61

Male and Female

Human beings are created male and female (see Gen. 1:27). This simple fact is a profound aspect of authentic humanity. God's glory is revealed in the distinctions between men and women, as well as in our unity as made in God's image. Because gender reflects the goodness of God's creation, we are to celebrate true masculinity and true femininity as gifts from God.

The biblical teachings on gender directly conflict with the thinking of the secular world, which increasingly sees gender differences as nothing more than socially constructed forms of oppression. Movements for normalizing transsexualism and transgender procedures represent forms of rebellion against God's purpose in creation. Gender chaos now prevails in much of our culture, leading to confusion and harm in the lives of individuals, families, and even churches. The creation of human beings as male and female and God's common affirmation of both genders demonstrate God's love for us and His design of different roles and responsibilities for men and women.

Fallen from Innocence

In the garden of Eden, Adam and Eve lived in the perfection of God's paradise on earth. Morally innocent, they did not sin and had no knowledge of sin. God commanded them to enjoy the fruit of the garden but forbade them to eat fruit from the tree of the knowledge of good and evil (see Gen. 2:16-17). As moral beings, Adam and Eve had the power of moral agency or choice, so they could choose whether to obey or disobey God.

> As moral beings, Adam and Eve had the power of moral agency or choice.

Then came temptation. When Adam and Eve ate the forbidden fruit, they disobeyed God and rebelled against His command (see Gen. 3:1-7). The consequences of their sin were incalculable. Because Adam was the head of the human race, humanity itself fell into sin and condemnation through his sin. Now that Adam and Eve were sinners, God justly cast them out of the garden (see Gen. 3:23-24). The consequences of their sin were truly catastrophic. With sin came sickness and death, and the earth itself became hostile to humanity (see Gen. 3:17-19). This biblical account is no myth. It is the historical account of humanity's fall from innocence into sin.

In the previous paragraph underline the consequences of Adam and Eve's sin.

Once Adam sinned, all humanity came under the condemnation of sin. From Adam the entire human race inherits a nature that is fallen and inclined toward sin. We are not born in a state of moral innocence; no human being after Adam is innocent. Though we still possess the capacity of moral agency, we must constantly choose between obedience and disobedience. As soon as we are morally able, we sin, break God's law, and come under God's condemnation for our own sin. This is not a pretty picture, but it is both real and honest. Without a clear diagnosis of our human condition as sinners, we cannot understand ourselves or realize our need for a Savior.

Restored to Fellowship with God

From the first moment of our lives, human beings are dependent creatures. As a matter of fact, a human infant is probably the most vulnerable, helpless, and defenseless being on earth. Even in our maturity we remain dependent on God for health, food, shelter, and protection. Just as we are dependent on God for the physical necessities of life, we are also spiritually helpless (see Rom. 5:6). Only God's plan of redemption allows us to have fellowship with God. Only by knowing Jesus Christ can we understand what true humanity was meant to be. By God's grace, demonstrated and made ours in Christ, we are restored to fellowship with God and are enabled to fulfill the purpose for which we were made.

God's love for us is seen most perfectly in Jesus Christ, whose atonement secures our salvation (see 1 Thess. 5:9). God decided to bring glory to His name by saving sinners, and He loved us so much that He gave His only Son for our redemption (see John 3:16). All who come to Christ by faith will be saved (see Rom. 10:13).

Christ's work of salvation includes men and women from every tribe, race, language, and people group: "You redeemed people for God by Your blood from every tribe and language and people and nation" (Rev. 5:9). This incredible fact should eliminate the possibility of racism or ethnic prejudice from God's people. Human beings are united in

"The meaning of the fall of humanity is that humanity sinned against God. Sin is not human infirmity merely, nor is it a mistake merely, nor is it ignorance merely. Sin, again, is not merely a step upward in humanity's evolution towards its highest development. The fall was a downward and not an upward movement of humanity. It involved guilt and transgression. It gave rise to the need of pardon, grace, and redemption."[3]

E. Y. Mullins
1860–1928
President, the Southern Baptist Theological Seminary

63

Christians must see every human being as made in God's image and as worthy of full respect and love.

our status as sinners who rightly come under God's condemnation. But all those who come to Christ by faith—drawn from every race and people—are united in God's new humanity. Therefore, Christians must see every human being as made in God's image and as worthy of full respect and love.

Read the following Scripture passages on humanity. Match each set of references with the correct summary statement.

___ 1. Genesis 1:26-27; James 3:9

___ 2. Psalm 51:5; Romans 3:10-12,23

___ 3. John 3:16; Romans 5:6-8

a. All have sinned.

b. People are made in God's image.

c. God loves us, and Christ died for our sins.

You should have matched the references this way: 1. b, 2. a, 3. c.

Because you are made in God's image, you have the capacity to know Him and worship Him. Answer these questions.

How well does my life reflect God's image?

_____

Do I enjoy daily fellowship with Him?	☐ Yes	☐ No
Do I maintain a consistent prayer life?	☐ Yes	☐ No
Do I have daily devotions?	☐ Yes	☐ No
Does biblical truth guide my thoughts and actions?	☐ Yes	☐ No
Do I spend time reflecting on my relationship with God?	☐ Yes	☐ No

How can I improve my relationship with God?

_____

CHAPTER 7
SALVATION

Article 4

Salvation

"Salvation involves the redemption of the whole man, and is offered freely to all who accept Jesus Christ as Lord and Saviour, who by His own blood obtained eternal redemption for the believer. In its broadest sense salvation includes regeneration, justification, sanctification, and glorification. There is no salvation apart from personal faith in Jesus Christ as Lord.

"A. Regeneration, or the new birth, is a work of God's grace whereby believers become new creatures in Christ Jesus. It is a change of heart wrought by the Holy Spirit through conviction of sin, to which the sinner responds in repentance toward God and faith in the Lord Jesus Christ. Repentance and faith are inseparable experiences of grace. Repentance is a genuine turning from sin toward God. Faith is the acceptance of Jesus Christ and commitment of the entire personality to Him as Lord and Saviour.

"B. Justification is God's gracious and full acquittal upon principles of His righteousness of all sinners who repent and believe in Christ. Justification brings the believer unto a relationship of peace and favor with God.

"C. Sanctification is the experience, beginning in regeneration, by which the believer is set apart to God's purposes, and is enabled to progress toward moral and spiritual maturity through the presence and power of the Holy Spirit dwelling in him. Growth in grace should continue throughout the regenerate person's life.

"D. Glorification is the culmination of salvation and is the final blessed and abiding state of the redeemed."[1]

> **Memory Verse**
>
> "God loved the world in this way: He gave His One and Only Son, so that everyone who believes in Him will not perish but have eternal life." John 3:16

Salvation is the great theme of the Bible. The central focus of the gospel message is the truth that God saves sinners. This is the greatest news the world has ever heard, and it is the very bedrock of the Christian faith.

God's Righteous Demands

Salvation
The process by which God redeems His creation through the life, death, and resurrection of His Son Jesus Christ

The Bible presents our salvation as rooted in the character of God. God is the loving Father who saves sinners, even as He is the Holy One of Israel who will judge with righteousness and perfect justice. The doctrine of salvation explains how God can be both just and the justifier of "the one who has faith in Jesus" (Rom. 3:26). God required a sacrifice for sin, but He also demonstrated His mercy by providing that sacrifice for sin—the only sacrifice that would meet the demands of His justice. This sacrifice is what the Bible means by *propitiation* (see Rom. 3:21-25). Jesus' death, burial, and resurrection frame the great events through which He purchased our salvation (see chap. 4).

Why was Jesus' death necessary for our salvation?

_____

_____

Only the sacrifice of God's perfect Son could satisfy God's righteous demand for justice and cancel the guilt of those who come to Him in faith.

Our Need

Our sin explains the need for God's work of salvation. Sin separated human beings from God, and God's judgment against sin created a barrier no human effort could overcome. As Isaiah said, all human attempts to achieve righteousness from the law are like filthy rags (see Isa. 64:6). Sinners cannot solve the problem of sin. As Paul described our plight, sinners are "dead in [our] trespasses and sins" (Eph. 2:1).

> "All of us have become like something unclean, and all our righteous acts are like a polluted garment."
> Isaiah 64:6

The following Scriptures deal with sin. Read them and match the references with the correct descriptions of sin.

___ 1. Isaiah 59:1-2

___ 2. Jeremiah 17:9

___ 3. John 3:18,36

___ 4. Romans 3:10-18,23

___ 5. James 4:17

___ 6. 1 John 3:4

a. Sin is universal; no one is righteous; everyone has turned away from God.

b. Unbelief in Jesus brings condemnation.

c. Sin builds barriers between us and God, and He hides His face from us.

d. Knowing to do good but not doing it is a sin.

e. Sin is breaking God's law.

f. The heart of a human being is deceitful and sick.

Mark each statement _T_ (true) or _F_ (false).

___ 1. The basic human problem is ignorance, not sin.

___ 2. Sin is universal among people.

___ 3. Sin is breaking God's law.

___ 4. Sin separates people from God.

___ 5. The root cause of sin is human weakness.

___ 6. Sin is willful rebellion against God.

___ 7. Sin is unbelief in Jesus as God's Son.

___ 8. Sin is against society, not against God.

___ 9. Sin is worshiping something other than God.

___ 10. People cannot deliver themselves from the power of sin.

The answers to the matching activity are 1. c, 2. f, 3. b, 4. a, 5. d, 6. e. Statements 1, 5, and 8 are false; 2, 3, 4, 6, 7, 9, and 10 are true.

Christ's Atonement

If God had not accomplished our salvation through Christ, that is where the human story would have ended—with sinners facing God's righteous wrath and without hope. But that's not the end of the story, and that's what makes the Christian gospel the greatest news ever known. As Paul explained, "God was in Christ reconciling the world to Himself" (2 Cor. 5:19; also see Mark 10:45; Luke 19:10; John 1:29).

The Bible also reveals the way God accomplished our salvation through Christ. The cross stands at the very center of the Christian faith. Christ's death was an atonement for sin: He died on the cross in the place of sinners. This is why we describe the work of Christ as *substitutionary* atonement. Put simply, Christ died in our place.

In His incarnation Jesus Christ was fully God and fully man. As the author of Hebrews explained, Jesus was "tested in every way as we are, yet without sin" (Heb. 4:15). His sinlessness is a vital part of the gospel story. His sinlessness also means that He perfectly fulfilled the law, thus canceling God's judgment against us. He triumphed over sin, death, and the curse.

Christ's atonement includes several important dimensions. Sinners are rescued, ransomed, purchased, and liberated from sin. But the concept of substitution stands at the very center. As Paul reminds us, "While we were still sinners Christ died for us!" (Rom. 5:8). Christ died for sinners and in the place of sinners. His death on the cross was penal in that He paid the penalty for our sins (see 1 Cor. 15:3).

"The Son of Man did not come to be served, but to serve, and to give His life—a ransom for many."
Mark 10:45

"The Son of Man has come to seek and to save the lost."
Luke 19:10

"Here is the Lamb of God, who takes away the sin of the world!"
John 1:29

"Christ died for our sins according to the Scriptures."
1 Corinthians 15:3

Choose the correct way to complete each sentence.
Christ's death on the cross was substitutionary because—
☐ He took the place of the Jewish high priest;
☐ He took our place;
☐ He took the place of the Passover lamb.
Christ's death on the cross was penal because—
☐ He paid the penalty for our sins;
☐ He died as our example.

68

On the cross Christ took our place and paid the penalty for our sins. *The Baptist Faith and Message* affirms that Jesus Christ obtained eternal redemption for believers "by His own blood." This is a very important affirmation, weaving together themes from the Old and New Testaments. In the Book of Leviticus, God instructed Israel that "the life of a creature is in the blood, and I have appointed it to you to make atonement on the altar for your lives, since it is the lifeblood that makes atonement" (Lev. 17:11). The Book of Hebrews makes this point even more emphatically: "According to the law almost everything is purified with blood, and without the shedding of blood there is no forgiveness" (Heb. 9:22).

The Book of Hebrews beautifully describes the meaning of Christ's death and atonement by explaining that Christ is our Great High Priest who entered the heavenly tabernacle and, just like the high priests of Israel in the earthy tabernacle, made atonement for sins through the sprinkling of blood. But unlike those human high priests, Jesus paid our penalty with His own blood, entering "the holy of holies once for all, … having obtained eternal redemption" (Heb. 9:12).

Those who deny the blood atonement deny the very center of the New Testament's presentation of God's gift of salvation. At the Last Supper, Jesus gave His disciples the cup, saying, "This is My blood that establishes the covenant; it is shed for many for the forgiveness of sins" (Matt. 26:28).

Stop and thank Jesus for shedding His blood on the cross for your sin.

The Only Way

The Baptist Faith and Message states that salvation "is offered freely to all who accept Jesus Christ as Lord and Saviour." Citing the prophet Joel, the Apostle Paul asserted, "Everyone who calls on the name of the Lord will be saved" (Rom. 10:13). In the most frequently cited verse in the Bible, Jesus told Nicodemus, "God loved the world in this way: He gave His One and Only Son, so that everyone who believes in Him will not perish but have eternal life" (John 3:16).

"[Faith] is always a volitional word. It is dynamic, never passive or lethargic. It moves; it marches; it is a commitment. … Faith is never intellectual assent or historical acknowledgment."[2]

W. A. Criswell
1909–2002
Pastor, First Baptist Church; Dallas, Texas

69

The crucial factor here is belief. Christians are believers in Christ; they believe what the Bible reveals about who He is, why He came, what He accomplished, and what this means for sinners. In other words, saving faith is a trusting faith, a belief that involves the total person, not merely the intellect.

Paul promised the Christians in Rome that "if you confess with your mouth, 'Jesus is Lord,' and believe in your heart that God raised Him from the dead, you will be saved" (Rom. 10:9). Believing with the heart—the very center of the human being—presents a wonderful definition of saving faith. W. T. Conner explained that faith "is assuming the attitude of entire dependence on God. Nothing else is faith. Refusing to assume this attitude is what keeps a man out of the kingdom of God."[3]

Salvation comes *only* to those who accept Jesus Christ as Savior and Lord. There is no other savior, and there is no other gospel that saves. Peter declared in Jerusalem, "There is salvation in no one else, for there is no other name under heaven given to people by which we must be saved" (Acts 4:12). Similarly, Jesus told Thomas, "I am the way, the truth, and the life. No one comes to the Father except through Me" (John 14:6). Thus, we cannot entertain the idea that there may be other ways of salvation. Jesus did not say, "I am *a* way." He said, "I am *the* way." There is no other way.

A lost world may label the Christian gospel as intolerant simply because the Bible teaches that Jesus Christ is the only Savior and that conscious faith in Christ is necessary for salvation. Nevertheless, we must oppose all forms of universalism and inclusivism while proclaiming the gospel that truly saves—and saves *all* who believe.

How would you respond to a neighbor asked you, "How can you say that Christ is the only way to salvation? There are many ways to God." What Scriptures could you use in your response?

> *"God has had one and only one plan of salvation for everybody everywhere—by grace alone, through faith alone, in Jesus Christ alone."[4]*
>
> Timothy George
> 1950–
> Founding dean,
> Beeson Divinity School,
> Samford University

Aspects of Salvation

The doctrine of salvation encompasses several important aspects of our redemption. All of these point to God's grace and mercy toward sinners.

Grace. Grace is one of the Bible's most beautiful words, reminding us that we are saved through God's unmerited favor. Grace affirms our absolute dependence on God. We do not deserve salvation, and we can do nothing to earn it. "By grace you are saved through faith," Paul instructs us, "and this is not from yourselves; it is God's gift—not from works, so that no one can boast" (Eph. 2:8-9).

Timothy George wrote, "There is a sense in which God's grace is so simple that even a small child can grasp its meaning. And yet it is so profound that the most learned theologians cannot fully comprehend its wonder and beauty and power."[5] George described the abundance of God's grace: "God's grace is inexhaustible, irrepressible, overflowing. God is not stingy. ... God's sufficient grace radiates its adequacy to meet the deepest needs of the vilest sinner who ever lived. There is no hell on earth so deep but that God's grace can go deeper still."[6]

Faith. Herschel Hobbs clearly illuminated the biblical meaning of *faith:* "Faith means to believe. But in its truest sense it is more than intellectual. It involves an act of the will whereby one trusts in Christ and commits one's self to him, to his will and way. It means to accept or receive Christ as both Lord and Savior. Thus one will be brought to confess him as such (Rom. 10:9-10)."[7]

Adrian Rogers explained the connection between grace and faith: "Here is how salvation works and the new birth comes about. I put my faith in God's grace. It is not the faith that saves; it is the grace that saves. Faith just lays hold of that grace. Think of grace as God's hand of love reaching down from heaven, saying, 'I love you. I want to save you.' It is a nail-pierced hand because He has paid for our sins. Think of faith as your sin-stained hand, saying, 'God, I need you. I want you.' And when you put your hand of faith in God's hand of grace, that is salvation."[8]

Grace
The unmerited favor of God that provides salvation

Faith
Belief in and personal commitment to Jesus Christ for eternal salvation

Regeneration
Spiritual rebirth

"Salvation, from its incipiency in the divine purpose before the world was created, to its consummation in glory, is all of grace."[9]
B. H. Carroll
1843–1914
Founder, Southwestern Baptist Theological Seminary

Regeneration. The Baptist Faith and Message defines *regeneration,* or the new birth, as the work of God's grace "whereby believers become new creatures in Christ Jesus." This concept explains why Christians often speak of being born again. Jesus Himself taught the biblical concept of the new birth; He told Nicodemus, "Unless someone is born again, he cannot see the kingdom of God" (John 3:3). Regeneration is the way God begins His work of salvation in us, and it explains why each Christian is a new creation in Christ (see 2 Cor. 5:17).

Peter tells us that we are born again "through the living and enduring word of God" (1 Pet. 1:23). He also tells us that God has given us "a new birth into a living hope through the resurrection of Jesus Christ from the dead" (1 Pet. 1:3).

Repentance. Repentance from sin is godly sorrow for sin—a genuine turning away from what had once ensnared us. Christ's saving work becomes evident in believers as they begin to hate the sin they had loved. In the Book of Acts the apostles affirmed the importance of repentance. On the day of Pentecost, Peter commanded the crowd: "Repent … and be baptized, each of you, in the name of Jesus the Messiah for the forgiveness of your sins" (Acts 2:38). At Mars Hill Paul warned the Athenians that "God now commands all people everywhere to repent" (Acts 17:30). Standing before King Agrippa, Paul defended the gospel, reminding the king that he had consistently called both Jews and Gentiles to "repent and turn to God" (Acts 26:20).

John Broadus defined *repentance* this way: "Repenting of sin means that one changes his thoughts and feelings about sin, resolving to forsake sin and live for God."[10] Lee Scarborough (1870–1945), the president of Southwestern Seminary from 1914 until his death in 1945, explained, "What is repentance? It is turning away from your sins. It is giving up the love of your sins, your affection for everything that you know to be wrong in your life. It is turning right about with a new view and a new vision of God."[11]

W. T. Conner showed the relationship between repentance and faith:

It is no accident that the experience of becoming a Christian has two fundamental aspects, for in this experience man is concerned with two fundamental relations of life. One is his relation to sin; the other, his relation to God as a God of grace, revealed in Christ as Saviour. The inward turning from sin is repentance; turning to Christ as Saviour is faith. Each implies the other. Neither is possible without the other. At the same time and in the same act that one turns from sin he turns to Christ. Sin and Christ are the opposite poles of the moral universe, and one cannot turn from one without turning to the other. Repentance and faith are not two acts or moral attitudes; they are two aspects of one act or attitude.[13]

Repentance
A change of heart and mind resulting in a turning from sin to God

Turn to *The Baptist Faith and Message* article on salvation, page 65. Fill in the blanks to define *regeneration, repentance,* and *faith.*

Regeneration, or the new _____, is a work of God's grace whereby believers become new _____ in Christ Jesus. It is a change of _____ wrought by the Holy Spirit through conviction of sin, to which the sinner responds in _____ toward God and _____ in the Lord Jesus Christ. Repentance and faith are inseparable experiences of _____. Repentance is a genuine _____ from sin toward God. Faith is the acceptance of Jesus Christ and commitment of the entire personality to Him as _____ and _____.

Read each Scripture. Match each reference with the term.

____ 1. Luke 15:17-18   a. Repentance
____ 2. Acts 2:38   b. Faith
____ 3. Acts 16:30-31
____ 4. Romans 10:8-10
____ 5. John 5:24
____ 6. Romans 2:4

You should have matched the verses 1. a, 2. a, 3. b, 4. b, 5. b, 6. a.

Justification
God's declaration of a believer as righteous through the blood of Christ

Sanctification
The position and process of holiness by which a believer is set apart by and for God

Glorification
The perfection of God's image and character in believers when they enter God's presence

Justification. Justification, as *The Baptist Faith and Message* states, "is God's gracious and full acquittal" of sinners who believe in Christ. W. A. Criswell explained, "In justification God declares that, on the basis of the atoning death of Christ to whom we are joined by faith, we have paid the penalty of the law for our sins—death. Jesus, to whom we are joined by faith, died for us so that the penalty has been paid. We are forgiven, justified, declared righteous."[14] John Dagg wrote,

Justification is the act of a judge acquitting one who is charged with crime. It is the opposite of condemnation. ... Justification is a higher blessing of grace, than pardon. The latter frees from the penalty due to sin, but it does not fully restore the lost favor of God. ... Such is the greatness of divine grace to the sinner who returns to God through Jesus Christ, that he is treated as if he had never sinned; and this is imported in the declaration that he is justified. ... Every penitent believer is both pardoned and justified. As repentance and faith are duties mutually implying each other, so pardon and justification are twin blessings of grace, bestowed together through Jesus Christ. All whom Jesus delivers from the wrath to come are freely justified from all things, and presented faultless before the presence of His glory.[15]

Incredibly, the Bible claims that God "justifies the ungodly" (Rom. 4:5, NASB). How can this be true? Can God truly justify the ungodly and remain holy and perfect? *The Baptist Faith and Message* stipulates that God's justification of sinners is accomplished "upon principles of His righteousness." In other words, God acts in a way that is perfectly consistent with His perfect character. In Romans 3:21-26 Paul shows us that, on the cross, God actually demonstrated His righteousness through the sacrifice of Christ.

Believers are justified by faith and by faith alone. We add nothing to the work of Christ, and our works amount to nothing. We are justified through faith alone as God's free and gracious gift is made ours by God's own declaration. *The Baptist Faith and Message* helpfully defines *saving faith* as "the acceptance of Jesus Christ and commitment of the entire personality to Him as Lord and Saviour."

Turn to *The Baptist Faith and Message* article on salvation, page 65. Fill in the blanks below to define *justification*.

Justification is God's gracious and full _____ upon principles of His _____ of all sinners who _____ and _____ in _____. Justification brings the believer unto a relationship of _____ and _____ with God.

Salvation involves the redemption of the whole person. It is not merely a cure for sin but the redemption of the entire sinner. The work of salvation that God has begun in all true believers will be fulfilled in the resurrection of our bodies and the completion of God's redemptive plan—a plan that includes past, present, and future dimensions.

Sanctification. Sanctification is the progressive work of the Holy Spirit by which, as *The Baptist Faith and Message* states, "the believer is set apart to God's purposes" and moves into Christian maturity. This work of God's grace begins at regeneration, when the new creation in Christ begins to grow in grace and to understand the things of God.

Sanctification explains how Christians grow into maturity and the fullness of the Christian life. Some denominations believe and teach that sanctification is an instantaneous event and that Christians can achieve moral and spiritual perfection in this life. Baptists do not share this belief. The Bible teaches us that the Christian life is an experience of growing in grace—moving from the elementary truths of God's Word into deeper truths (see Heb. 5:12-14). Christians are instructed to grow toward maturity in order to serve the cause of Christ, but full maturity must await the glorification that Christ will accomplish in believers in the age to come (see Phil. 1:6).

Glorification. Glorification completes the saving work of God. *The Baptist Faith and Message* states that it is "the culmination of salvation and is the final blessed and abiding state of the redeemed." Paul

"Though by this time you ought to be teachers, you have need again for someone to teach you the elementary principles of the oracles of God, and you have come to need milk and not solid food. For everyone who partakes only of milk is not accustomed to the word of righteousness, for he is an infant. But solid food is for the mature, who because of practice have their senses trained to discern good and evil."
Hebrews 5:12-14

"He who began a good work in you will perfect it until the day of Christ Jesus."
Philippians 1:6

75

encouraged Christians to look with anticipation to the "eternal weight of glory" that is promised to believers (2 Cor. 4:17).

Our glorification awaits Christ's appearing.

Our glorification awaits Christ's appearing. John promised believers that when Christ appears, we will be like Him: "We are God's children now, and what we will be has not yet been revealed. We know that when He appears, we will be like Him, because we will see Him as He is" (1 John 3:2).

Underline the definitions of *sanctification* and *glorification* in the previous paragraphs.

Read each passage and match the reference with the aspect of salvation to which it primarily refers.

___ 1. Romans 8:17 a. Regeneration
___ 2. 2 Timothy 2:21 b. Justification
___ 3. John 3:3-6 c. Sanctification
___ 4. Colossians 1:9-10 d. Glorification
___ 5. 1 Corinthians 15:52-53
___ 6. Romans 5:1
___ 7. Romans 3:23-24
___ 8. Titus 3:5

The correct answers are 1. d, 2. c, 3. a, 4. c, 5. d, 6. b, 7. b. 8. a.

If an unsaved person asked you how to be saved, what would you say? Write some ideas about each subject on a separate sheet of paper.

- Sin
- God's love
- The cross
- Faith
- Repentance

Write at least one Scripture reference beside each point in the outline. Practice sharing your outline with a family member of a friend. Ask God to give you opportunities to share His salvation with lost persons.

CHAPTER 8

GOD'S PURPOSE OF GRACE

Article 5

God's Purpose of Grace

"Election is the gracious purpose of God, according to which He regenerates, justifies, sanctifies, and glorifies sinners. It is consistent with the free agency of man, and comprehends all the means in connection with the end. It is the glorious display of God's sovereign goodness, and is infinitely wise, holy, and unchangeable. It excludes boasting and promotes humility.

"All true believers endure to the end. Those whom God has accepted in Christ, and sanctified by His Spirit, will never fall away from the state of grace, but shall persevere to the end. Believers may fall into sin through neglect and temptation, whereby they grieve the Spirit, impair their graces and comforts, and bring reproach on the cause of Christ and temporal judgments on themselves; yet they shall be kept by the power of God through faith unto salvation."[1]

> **Memory Verses**
> "My sheep hear My voice, I know them, and they follow Me.
> I give them eternal life, and they will never perish—ever!
> No one will snatch them out of My hand. My Father, who
> has given them to Me, is greater than all. No one is able
> to snatch them out of the Father's hand." John 10:27-29

Salvation begins in the eternal purpose of God—His determination to save sinners through the atonement accomplished by Jesus Christ, His Son. This is important for Christians to know because it secures our salvation in God's power and purpose rather than in our own efforts. This great truth also reminds Christians that God's plan to save sinners began before the creation of the world. Jesus Christ is the Lamb of God, slain "from the foundation of the world" (Rev. 13:8).

The Gracious Purpose of God

Election is a central doctrine of the Bible, affirming that God saves sinners. As *The Baptist Faith and Message* defines this doctrine, "Election is the gracious purpose of God, according to which He regenerates, justifies, sanctifies, and glorifies sinners." In other words, the doctrine of election explains how God's grace brings salvation to His people.

Election
God's gracious action in choosing people to follow Him and obey His commands

God announced to the children of Israel His purpose to redeem a people and constantly reminded them that they were a chosen people, an elect nation. God chose Israel from among all the nations of the earth to show the power of His name. Israel heard God's voice (see Deut. 4:33) and received the law, supremely revealed in the Ten Commandments (see Ex. 20:1-18). God did not choose Israel because the nation was wealthy, numerous, or powerful but because He willed to take a tiny nation, make it great, and show His glory through the people He had chosen (see Deut. 7:7-8; Isa. 44:1; 45:4).

Israel became the people through whom God would send the Messiah, the Savior of the world. Israel's special status and national privilege were to be the people through whom God would bless all nations. The Lord told Abraham, "All the nations of the earth will be blessed by your offspring because you have obeyed My command" (Gen. 22:18).

Because Israel broke the original covenant with God, the prophet Jeremiah announced the promise of a new covenant (see Jer. 31:31-34). Jesus is the fulfillment of that covenant. At the Last Supper Jesus said to His followers, "This cup is the new covenant established by My blood; it is shed for you" (Luke 22:20). God's redemptive purpose is fulfilled in the church, His redeemed people who have been bought with a price—the blood of the Lord Jesus Christ. Election affirms that God took the initiative in our salvation.

Read John 6:37,44. Then write your own paraphrase.

_____

_____

What is God's purpose for humankind?

_____

"Everyone the Father gives Me will come to Me, and the one who comes to Me I will never cast out. No one can come to Me unless the Father who sent Me draws him, and I will raise him up on the last day."
John 6:37,44

You may have written something like this: "The ones given to Jesus by the Father will never be turned away, and no one can come to Jesus unless the Father draws him." God takes the initiative to bring about His purpose to save people.

The atonement Christ accomplished was not a plan God put into effect after observing human sinfulness. On the contrary, God determined to save sinners, and He does so in a manner consistent with His power, authority, righteousness, justice, mercy, and love. One paraphrase renders Ephesians 1:11-12 in a striking manner: "It's in Christ that we find out who we are and what we are living for. Long before we first heard of Christ and got our hopes up, He had His eye on us, had designs on us for glorious living, part of the overall purpose He is working out in everything and everyone."[2] God's plan of salvation is perfect, and He remains sovereign throughout the unfolding of human history and His dealings with humankind.

The Free Agency of Man

The Baptist Faith and Message also affirms that God's purpose of grace "is consistent with the free agency of man." In other words, the statement affirms human freedom and responsibility. As Herschel Hobbs commented, "Two truths, therefore, must be recognized in regard to election: God's sovereignty and man's free will. Both are abundantly taught in the Bible."[3] Baptists gladly affirm both truths—that God is sovereign and that human beings are given free agency and personal responsibility. These two truths are difficult for our finite minds to understand. Charles Spurgeon even questioned whether we would be able to reconcile the truths in heaven! "I am not sure that in heaven we shall be able to know where the free agency of man and the sovereignty of God meet, but both are great truths."[4]

Throughout the history of the church, Christians have struggled to find the best way to reconcile God's sovereignty and humanity's free will. Although Baptists have included believers who hold different understandings of how these truths are to be affirmed, we stand together on the great truth that God alone saves sinners. We are united in affirming both divine sovereignty and human responsibility. This is our common faith. We can exclaim with Paul,

God alone saves sinners.

> Oh, the depth of the riches
> both of the wisdom and the knowledge
>   of God!
> How unsearchable His judgments
> and untraceable His ways!
> Romans 11:33

Read the following Scripture verses. Write the references in the proper columns to indicate whether the verses emphasize God's sovereignty or humans' free will.

John 3:15-16; John 5:24; John 15:16,19; Acts 13:48; Romans 8:29-30; Romans 10:9-13; 1 Thessalonians 5:9; 2 Thessalonians 2:13-14; Revelation 22:17

God's Sovereignty	Humans' Free Will
_____	_____
_____	_____
_____	_____
_____	_____
_____	_____

God's sovereignty: John 15:16,19; Acts 13:48; Romans 8:29-30; 1 Thessalonians 5:9; 2 Thessalonians 2:13-14.

Humans' free will: John 3:15-16; John 5:24; Romans 10:9-13; Revelation 22:17.

The Baptist Faith and Message also points to the most important truth about the gospel: it is "the glorious display of God's sovereign goodness." The gospel is indeed directed to sinners, but God's ultimate purpose is to reveal His character as the God who redeems, saves, and forgives sinners.

There is no room for human boasting in God's redemptive plan. Spurgeon wrote, "Election, to a saint, is one of the most *stripping* doctrines in all the world—to take away all trust in the flesh, or all reliance upon anything except Jesus Christ. How often do we wrap ourselves up in our own righteousness, and array ourselves with the false pearls and gems of our own works and doings. We begin to say 'Now I shall be saved, because I have this and that evidence.' Instead of that, it is naked faith that saves; that faith and that alone unites to the Lamb, irrespective of works, although it is productive of them."[5]

Enduring to the End

We are to find great comfort and confidence in the promise that God's saving purpose is unchangeable. E. Y. Mullins wrote, "Election ... does, when truly understood, fill us with humility and a sense of the manifold wisdom of God in dealing with His free creatures."[7] God's character is constant, and His power is unlimited. As Paul encouraged the Romans, we are to find assurance in the fact that nothing can separate believers from the love of God (see Rom. 8:38-39).

This is incredibly good news. God's purposes cannot be thwarted, and no power can snatch believers out of the Lord's hand. As Jesus told His disciples, "My Father, who has given them to Me, is greater than all. No one is able to snatch them out of the Father's hand" (John 10:29). In Isaiah 40 the prophet wrote about God's power and greatness. He asked, "Who has measured the waters in the hollow of his hand?" (Isa. 40:12). The obvious implication is that God has done so. The psalmist wrote, "The depths of the earth are in His hand" (Ps. 95:4). The great God of the universe who holds the mighty oceans in the palm of His hand also holds believers in Christ securely in His hand.

All true believers endure to the end because their salvation is secure in Christ. Christians must accept the vital promise that God's saving purpose will be completed in us. Paul expressed a similar confidence

"It [election] prostrates all human hope at the feet of a Sovereign God, and teaches the prayer, 'Lord, if Thou wilt, Thou canst make me clean.' It discountenances all effort to save ourselves by our own works of righteousness; but brings the sinner to commit himself at once to the sovereign mercy of God."[6]

John Dagg
Baptist pastor, teacher, and administrator

"This doctrine of the safety of the child of God encourages the holiest of living among God's children for it has behind it the holiest and mightiest of all motives that control the hearts of men and women. It has behind it the great motive of love. If I can be saved by the grace of God and He is responsible for my salvation and He has given me His word that He will save me and all we are to do is to leave it to Him, out of love and gratitude to Him, I will give Him the deepest and most consecrated service of my life for what He has done for me."[8]

M. E. Dodd
1878–1952
Pastor, First Baptist Church; Shreveport, Louisiana; president, Southern Baptist Convention, 1934–35

to the Philippians, encouraging them with these words: "I am sure of this, that He who started a good work in you will carry it on to completion until the day of Christ Jesus" (Phil. 1:6).

Southern Baptists have always been absolutely united in affirming that all true believers will endure to the end. This assurance is another dimension of God's grace. We are saved by grace, transformed by grace, and kept by grace as God's gift of salvation is made ours by faith. Believers are secure because nothing—and no one—can separate us from the love of God. God keeps His own and loses none.

Read the following Scripture passages, all related to the believer's security in Christ. Match each one with the correct summary statement.

___ 1. 2 Timothy 1:12	a. We are protected by God's power.
___ 2. Philippians 1:6	b. The life Jesus imparts to us is eternal.
___ 3. Hebrews 7:25	c. We can know our salvation is secure.
___ 4. John 5:24	d. Jesus has promised never to forsake us.
___ 5. 1 Peter 1:3-5	e. God finishes what He begins.
___ 6. Hebrews 13:5	f. Jesus intercedes for us.

The verses should be matched this way: 1. c, 2. e, 3. f, 4. b, 5. a, 6. d.

Eternal security does not mean that all who claim to believe in Jesus will be saved. The New Testament contains many warnings about false belief and false believers. Jesus spoke of the human heart in terms of four soils, warning that the shallow soil appears to receive the seed of the gospel, but no real life endures (see Matt. 13:1-23; Luke 8:4-15). Some claim to follow Christ but fall away and even repudiate the faith. How do we know that these persons were never true believers? John answered that question by explaining, "They went out from us, but they did not belong to us; for if they had belonged to us, they would have remained with us. However, they went out so that it might be made clear that none of them belongs to us" (1 John 2:19).

The Baptist Faith and Message emphasizes that true Christians are those who "persevere to the end." The perseverance of believers is the evidence of true and authentic faith—faith that saves. Thus, true believers "will never fall away from the state of grace." Having been accepted by God in Christ, believers are being sanctified by the power of God. This is a lifelong process that begins with our salvation but is fully accomplished only in our glorification that is to come.

Believers sin and may even fall into grave and awful sin that brings disrepute on themselves and the church. True believers can never remain in such a state of sin and rebellion but will repent. Peter instructed believers to "make your calling and election sure" (2 Pet. 1:3). This should encourage Christians to look carefully at our lives, knowing that Christ taught believers to be fruitful and faithful.

In the end, however, our confidence is not in ourselves or even in our own faithfulness. Our confidence is in God and in God's promises to us. Christians are "protected by the power of God through faith for a salvation to be revealed in the last time" (1 Pet. 1:5). Kept by the power of God, Christians have nothing to fear. In some well-known verses the Apostle Paul demonstrated this same confidence.

Read Romans 8:38-39 in the margin. Underline the 10 things that cannot separate a believer from God's love.

John Dagg cautioned against misusing the teaching of the eternal security of the believer: "The doctrine of final perseverance, properly understood, gives no encouragement to sluggishness or negligence in duty; much less does it lead to licentiousness. He who takes occasion from it to sin against God, or to be indolent in his service, not only misunderstands, and misapplies the doctrine, but has reason to fear that his heart is not right before God."[9]

Believers are encouraged to trust securely and safely in Christ. In one sense assurance is a Christian duty, for to doubt our salvation is to doubt God's promises. God's purpose of grace reminds us that grace explains the entirety of our salvation, from beginning to end. We are saved, preserved, protected, and secured by the grace of God. This is God's perfect purpose.

Security of the Believer
The doctrine teaching that true believers are eternally saved and therefore secure in their salvation

"Neither death
nor life,
nor angels
nor rulers,
nor things present,
nor things to come,
nor powers,
nor height,
nor depth,
nor any other
created thing
will have the power
to separate us
from the love of
God that is in Christ
Jesus our Lord!"
Romans 8:38-39

Review by marking each statement *T* (true) or *F* (false).

___ 1. Salvation begins in God's eternal purpose to save sinners through Christ.

___ 2. God's plan to save sinners came before the creation of the world.

___ 3. God is sovereign in His dealings with humankind.

___ 4. Human beings possess free will; they can accept or reject God's offer of salvation.

___ 5. Baptists affirm both divine sovereignty and human responsibility in salvation.

___ 6. All true believers endure to the end and are eternally secure.

___ 7. All who claim to believe in Jesus will be saved.

___ 8. The perseverance of believers is the evidence of true faith.

___ 9. True believers cannot sin.

___ 10. The doctrine of final perseverance encourages us to be lax in Christian living.

Statements 1, 2, 3, 4, 5, 6, and 8 are true; 7, 9, and 10 are false.

State one new thing you have learned in this chapter.

_____

_____

_____

Ask God to help you serve Him with greater confidence and assurance because of the eternal security of your salvation.

CHAPTER 9

THE CHURCH

Article 6

The Church

"A New Testament church of the Lord Jesus Christ is an autonomous local congregation of baptized believers, associated by covenant in the faith and fellowship of the gospel; observing the two ordinances of Christ, governed by His laws, exercising the gifts, rights, and privileges invested in them by His Word, and seeking to extend the gospel to the ends of the earth. Each congregation operates under the Lordship of Christ through democratic processes. In such a congregation each member is responsible and accountable to Christ as Lord. Its scriptural officers are pastors and deacons. While both men and women are gifted for service in the church, the office of pastor is limited to men as qualified by Scripture.

"The New Testament speaks also of the church as the Body of Christ which includes all of the redeemed of all the ages, believers from every tribe, and tongue, and people, and nation."[1]

Memory Verse

"He is also the head of the body, the church;

He is the beginning, the firstborn from the dead,

so that He might come to have first place in everything."

Colossians 1:18

The New Testament church—the body and bride of Christ—stands at the very center of God's redemptive work. Baptists are shaped by a strong, vibrant New Testament vision of the church as the people of God—a holy people and a people on mission.

The Foundation of the Church

> "No one can lay any other foundation than what has been laid—that is, Jesus Christ."
>
> 1 Corinthians 3:11

The foundation of the church is Jesus Christ (see 1 Cor. 3:11). Paul wrote that the church is "built on the foundation of the apostles and prophets, with Christ Jesus Himself as the cornerstone" (Eph. 2:20). Thus, Jesus Christ is the Lord over His church, and His saving work is the foundation of the church itself. M. E. Dodd wrote, "The deity of Jesus, His virgin birth, His vicarious atonement, His bodily resurrection and His second coming are the component parts of this foundation. ... The church has a sure foundation, a safe foundation, a solid foundation, an enduring foundation, an eternal foundation."[2]

In Matthew 16:13-19, often called the Great Constitution, Jesus declared the establishment of the church and instructed the disciples about its meaning. After Peter had confessed Jesus as "the Messiah, the Son of the living God!" (v. 16), Jesus told him, "I also say to you that you are Peter, and on this rock I will build My church, and the forces of Hades will not overpower it" (v. 18). Jesus clearly stated that the church is established not on Peter but on Peter's confession that Jesus is the Christ, the Son of the living God. This is the confession of all true Christians, and it is the great foundation on which the church stands. Jesus promised His church that not even death (Hades) could prevail against it. In other words, the church will survive even death.

The Body of Christ

Church
The community of those who believe in and follow Jesus Christ

The Greek word *ekklesia,* the primary New Testament word for *church,* means *the ones called out.* Christians are called out from the world into the fellowship of the church. The called-out ones are visible in local congregations that are part of the body of Christ.

Read Ephesians 1:20-23 and Colossians 1:18 in the margin on the following page. The head of the church is—
☐ the pastor; ☐ Christ; ☐ the deacons; ☐ the members.

Read in your Bible 1 Corinthians 12:12-27, in which Paul used the analogy of the human body to describe the church. After each statement write the number of the verse that supports that statement.

1. The same Holy Spirit is at work in all believers, and the church transcends ethnic and social differences. Verse _____

2. Paul used the figure of the human body with its many different members yet with a basic unity to illustrate the body of Christ. Verse _____

3. Each individual member of the body is a part of the body and belongs in the body. Verse _____

4. The church is the body of Christ. Verse _____

5. God has placed each member in the body according to His plan. Verse _____

6. Christians with more obvious gifts should not look down on less gifted believers. Verse _____

7. When one member suffers, the whole body is involved. Members should show concern for one another. Verse _____

Here is how we matched the verses with the statements: 1. verse 13, 2. verse 12, 3. verses 15-17, 4. verse 27, 5. verse 18, 6. verse 21, 7. verse 26.

Read Romans 12:4-8. This passage describes different functions or gifts of the members of the body of Christ. Then complete the following list. The first entry is completed for you.

If the gift is:	Use it this way:
Prophecy	*According to the standard of faith*
Service	_____
Teaching	_____
Exhorting	_____
Giving	_____
Leading	_____
Showing mercy	_____

"He demonstrated this power in the Messiah by raising Him from the dead and seating Him at His right hand in the heavens—far above every ruler and authority, power and dominion, and every title given, not only in this age but also in the one to come. And He put everything under His feet and appointed Him as head over everything for the church, which is His body, the fullness of the One who fills all things in every way."
Ephesians 1:20-23

"He is also the head of the body, the church; He is the beginning, the firstborn from the dead, so that He might come to have first place in everything."
Colossians 1:18

87

The vast majority of New Testament references to the church refer to local congregations, but *The Baptist Faith and Message* also affirms the church as "the Body of Christ which includes all of the redeemed of all the ages, believers from every tribe, and tongue, and people, and nation" (see Rev. 5:9). Thus, the church has both local and universal meanings. However, the New Testament primarily focuses on the local congregation as the visible representation of the church.

Characteristics of the Church

Autonomy. The Baptist Faith and Message identifies the local church as "an autonomous local congregation of baptized believers." This means that every local congregation is invested with full authority to fulfill its ministry. Baptists do not believe in a hierarchical system above the local church because none is found in the New Testament. No earthly headquarters can exert authority over the local church.

Jesus' lordship. Baptists rightly prize the autonomous nature of local congregations, but we stand with all Christians in affirming the lordship of Jesus Christ over His church. The church serves the resurrected and reigning Lord Jesus Christ. Christ rules in His church through the ministry of the Word and the guidance of the Holy Spirit. He exercises His authority in the church by means of New Testament principles handed down to the apostles and through them to the church. Each congregation must organize its ministry so that Christ's rule and reign are evident in its life and work. Because every baptized believer is empowered to fully take part in church life, a local church works through democratic processes under the lordship of Christ.

Covenant
A contract or agreement expressing God's gracious promises to His people and their consequent relationship to Him

Covenant. The concept of covenant lies at the heart of the Baptist vision of the church. A church is not merely a voluntary association or a social organization. Instead, it is a congregation of believers who covenant together to fulfill Christ's ministry. The idea of covenant has a rich heritage, for in the Old Testament God made a series of covenants with His people (see Gen. 9:8-17; 17:1-22; Ex. 24:1-8; Jer. 31:31-34). A covenant binds church members to one another in a sacred bond of love and mutual accountability before Christ. Members pledge to one another their trust, their faith, and their eagerness to work together for the glory of Christ. The local church is a covenant community of believers who, united by a common faith and a saving experience with the Lord Jesus Christ, willingly enter a covenant together to fulfill all the responsibilities and receive all the promises God gives His people.

Baptized believers. The *Baptist Faith and Message* states that a local church is a congregation of baptized believers. Baptism is the believer's public profession of faith in Christ, a sign and symbol of the new birth. Our common baptism binds us together as believers and establishes the boundary of membership in the congregation.

Read each Scripture reference and match it with the correct summary statement.

___ 1. Matthew 16:13-19
___ 2. Acts 6:1-3
___ 3. Acts 13:1-3
___ 4. Ephesians 2:19-22
___ 5. Colossians 1:18
___ 6. 1 Peter 5:1-4
___ 7. Revelation 2:1-3

a. The pastor is not to lord over church members but to be an example.
b. The Holy Spirit speaks to and through the church.
c. Most likely refers to the origin of the office of deacon.
d. Jesus said He would build His church.
e. Christ knows the works of a church.
f. Christ is the Head of the church.
g. The church is compared to a building.

You probably matched the verses and statements this way: 1. d, 2. c, 3. b, 4. g, 5. f, 6. a, 7. e.

The Ministry of the Church

Our Lord left His church a specific blueprint for the way congregations are to organize and fulfill His Great Commission (see Matt. 28:19-20) and His Great Commandment (see Mark 12:30). Christian churches

"Go, therefore, and make disciples of all nations, baptizing them in the name of the Father and of the Son and of the Holy Spirit, teaching them to observe everything I have commanded you. And remember, I am with you always, to the end of the age."
Matthew 28:19-20

"Love the Lord your God with all your heart, with all your soul, with all your mind, and with all your strength."
Mark 12:30

89

"The Spirit and the bride say, 'Come!' Anyone who hears should say, 'Come!' And the one who is thirsty should come. Whoever desires should take the living water as a gift."
Revelation 22:17

"The church, like individual Christians, is the salt of the earth; is the light of the world; is a city that is set on a hill and cannot be hid; and has the glorious privilege of letting its light so shine before men that they may see the good works and glorify God."[3]
J. M. Frost
1848–1916
Founding secretary, the Sunday School Board (now LifeWay Christian Resources) of the Southern Baptist Convention

are obligated to obey the law of Christ and to exercise all the gifts, rights, and privileges the Lord grants believers through His Word. Central to this assignment is the task of gospel witness to the ends of the earth. There are no geographical limits on the local church's gospel responsibility, even as the church ministers to its own community.

Read Revelation 22:17. The church's primary mission is—
- ☐ to invite every person to come to Christ;
- ☐ to observe the ordinances Christ commanded;
- ☐ to eradicate poverty and human suffering.

Read *The Baptist Faith and Message* article on the church, page 85, and underline the church's missionary task.

The marks of a church include preaching the Word, observing the ordinances, disciplining its members, and ministering according to God's Word. Worship stands at the forefront of the church's ministry, and preaching stands at the forefront of worship. A true gospel church places a high priority on preaching and teaching. The congregation is also commanded to hold members accountable to Christ's commands as revealed in His Word and to seek to restore members to full fellowship when sin or a breech in fellowship divides or harms the church and its members (see Matt. 18:15-17; Gal. 6:1).

The Baptist Faith and Message states that in a New Testament church each member "is responsible and accountable to Christ as Lord." Every believer has a task to fulfill and spiritual gifts to share (see Rom. 12:6-8; 1 Cor. 12:7-12,28-30). The New Testament gives no support to spectator Christianity. Christians are to invest themselves in the ministry of the local congregation, finding and filling roles of service, leadership, and ministry.

The Structure of the Church

The New Testament provides a blueprint for church structure. The scriptural officers of the church are pastors and deacons. Paul mentioned these officers in the greeting of his letter to the Philippians (see Phil. 1:1).

90

Pastor. The New Testament words that Baptists identify with the pastoral office include terms translated as *bishop, elder,* and *pastor.* Each term adds to our understanding of the pastoral office and the pastor's responsibility. *Bishop* means *overseer*—someone who oversees the work of others. Jews used the word *elder* to designate someone who possessed dignity and wisdom. In the Christian church *elder* was used for someone who presided over assemblies and served as a counselor. The term *pastor* describes a shepherd who loves and cares for the believers who make up the congregation (see Acts 20:28).[4]

Baptists do not believe that the New Testament establishes a role for a bishop over several churches. Instead, the Bible says every pastor is to serve as a bishop who exercises and fulfills the ministry of the Word on behalf of the congregation as the gathered people of God.

Central to the pastor's role is the responsibility to preach and teach. Paul instructed Timothy, "Preach the Word; be ready in season and out of season; reprove, rebuke, exhort, with great patience and understanding" (2 Tim. 4:2). Above all else, the pastor must preach and teach the Word of God.

We also affirm that the office of pastor is limited to men as qualified by Scripture. This assertion has become controversial only in recent years. Until recently, all Christians affirmed that the pastoral office is limited to men recognized as fully qualified by biblical definitions. The Bible clearly reveals a complementary relationship between men and women. Both are equally created in the image of God (see Gen. 1:27; Gal. 3:28). Both are gifted for service in the church. But the New Testament defines a pastor as a man who is "the husband of one wife" (1 Tim. 3:2) and a man who is gifted by God to fulfill the pastoral role. God's instruction is for men to assume and fulfill the preaching ministry. Many other ministries and responsibilities are available in the church for both men and women. As Christ made abundantly clear, there is no shortage of work for His disciples to do.

Deacon. The other local New Testament church officer is the deacon, who is to serve the church through ministry so that pastors can devote themselves to the teaching and preaching of the Word (see Acts 6:3-6).

"To all the saints in Christ Jesus who are in Philippi, including the overseers and deacons."
Philippians 1:1

"Be on guard for yourselves and for all the flock, among whom the Holy Spirit has appointed you as overseers, to shepherd the church of God, which He purchased with His own blood."
Acts 20:28

Bishop
An overseer

Elder
An adviser and counselor

Pastor
The shepherd of a flock

Deacon
An office in the church that involves ministry and service

"Deacons ... should be worthy of respect, not hypo-critical, not drinking a lot of wine, not greedy for money, holding the mystery of the faith with a clear conscience. ... Deacons must be husbands of one wife, managing their children and their own house-holds competently. For those who have served well as deacons acquire a good standing for themselves, and great boldness in the faith that is in Christ Jesus."
1 Timothy 3:8-13

The Bible sets a high standard for deacons, specifying many of the same qualifications as for pastors (see 1 Tim. 3:8-13).

Mark each statement *T* (true) or *F* (false).
___ 1. The congregation is autonomous—its own self-determining body.
___ 2. There is no hierarchical system above a local Baptist church.
___ 3. The pastor is the Head of the church.
___ 4. The local Baptist association exerts authority over a local Baptist church in that association.
___ 5. Every local church has full authority to fulfill its ministry.
___ 6. The local church works through democratic processes under the lordship of Christ.
___ 7. The terms *bishop, elder,* and *pastor* all refer to the pastoral office, not to three separate offices.
___ 8. Men and women are gifted for service in the church.
___ 9. Scripture limits the office of pastor to men.

Statements 1, 3, and 4 are false; 2, 5, 6, 7, 8, and 9 are true. Statement 1 is false because Jesus Christ is the Lord of the church, and the church should seek His will.

Check the two scriptural officers in a church.
☐ pastor   ☐   trustee   ☐ teacher   ☐ deacon

State two actions you can take to strengthen the ministry of your church.

1. _____

2. _____

Pray for your pastor and deacons, your church staff and leaders, and your church's ministry.

CHAPTER 10
BAPTISM AND THE LORD'S SUPPER

Article 7
Baptism and the Lord's Supper

"Christian baptism is the immersion of a believer in water in the name of the Father, the Son, and the Holy Spirit. It is an act of obedience symbolizing the believer's faith in a crucified, buried, and risen Saviour, the believer's death to sin, the burial of the old life, and the resurrection to walk in newness of life in Christ Jesus. It is a testimony to his faith in the final resurrection of the dead. Being a church ordinance, it is prerequisite to the privileges of church membership and to the Lord's Supper.

"The Lord's Supper is a symbolic act of obedience whereby members of the church, through partaking of the bread and the fruit of the vine, memorialize the death of the Redeemer and anticipate His second coming."[1]

Memory Verse

"If anyone is in Christ, there is a new creation; old things have passed away, and look, new things have come."

2 Corinthians 5:17

Ordinance
A decree or
command

Christ assigned His church two ordinances—baptism and the Lord's Supper. *Ordinance* means *decree* or *command*. Baptists refer to baptism and the Lord's Supper as ordinances that are commanded by Christ. Other denominations view these acts as sacraments. The word *sacrament* implies that the act itself conveys grace to the believer. Baptists believe that Christ gave baptism and the Lord's Supper to His church not as sacraments but as pictures and affirmations of grace .

Draw lines to connect *symbol* and *sacrament* with their correct definitions.

| Symbol | A Christian rite as a means of grace |
| Sacrament | A Christian rite as a picture |

An ordinance is   ☐ a command   ☐ a sacrament.

Baptists observe the ordinances of baptism and the Lord's Supper because Christ commanded us to. Our faithful obedience to Christ's commands testifies of God's grace. The ordinances are thus illustrations and remembrances of grace and sources of blessing to believers. They do not bestow sacramental grace on the participants or on the observing congregation. Rather, believers receive grace and blessing when we obey Christ's commands and remember His saving acts.

Baptism

Baptize
Submerge, plunge,
or immerse

The Bible clearly defines *baptism* as the immersion of believers in water. Baptism is not a denominational eccentricity. Believers' baptism by immersion is deeply rooted in the nature of the ordinance and in the picture that immersion provides the church. The Greek word used in the New Testament for *baptism, baptizo*, is most clearly understood to mean submersion in water—the complete immersion of an object or, in this case, a person in water. Sprinkling and partial immersion do not satisfy the New Testament definition of *baptism*.

In fulfillment of the Great Commission, Baptists baptize "in the name of the Father and of the Son and of the Holy Spirit" (Matt. 28:19). Thus, baptism is a trinitarian act, reminding believers that our salvation has been promised, accomplished, and applied through the work of the one true God—Father, Son, and Holy Spirit.

A believer's immersion in water pictures the death, burial, and resurrection of Christ, providing a beautiful picture of our salvation and reminding us of His saving work (see Rom. 6:4). The picture of life from death is a powerful witness of the gospel and of the promises the Father made to the Son in the covenant of redemption.

Baptism pictures a believer's death to sin and his resurrection to walk in newness of life. Lee Scarborough wrote, "He publicly puts a grave between himself and his former life of sin."[2] The scriptural testimony about this act is rich and powerful. Baptism depicts the complete surrender of life and the transformation only Christ can bring. Through it a believer publicly professes faith in Christ.

> "We were buried with Him by baptism into death, in order that, just as Christ was raised from the dead by the glory of the Father, so we too may walk in a new way of life."
> Romans 6:4

Mark each statement _T_ (true) or _F_ (false).

_____ 1. The mode or form of baptism is not important.

_____ 2. Baptists practice baptism by immersion because of tradition.

_____ 3. The Greek word for _baptism_ refers to complete immersion in water.

_____ 4. We are commanded to baptize in the name of the Father, Son, and Holy Spirit.

_____ 5. A believer publicly professes faith in Christ by the act of baptism.

_____ 6. Baptism pictures a believer's death to sin and his resurrection to walk in newness of life.

_____ 7. Baptism pictures Christ's death, burial, and resurrection.

_____ 8. Scripture presents sprinkling as a legitimate mode of baptism.

Statements 1, 2, and 8 are false; 3, 4, 5, 6, and 7 are true.

Baptism uniquely pictures Paul's description of a believer as a living sacrifice (see Rom. 12:1). Being dead to self and alive to Christ is nowhere more perfectly pictured than in the ordinance of baptism,

> "Present your bodies as a living sacrifice, holy and pleasing to God; this is your spiritual worship."
> Romans 12:1

*"We sink beneath
the water's face,
And thank You for
Your saving grace;
We die to sin and
seek a grave
With You, beneath
the yielding wave.
And as we rise
with You to live,
O let the Holy
Spirit give
The sealing unction
from above,
The joy of life,
the fire of love."*[3]

Adoniram Judson
1788–1850
The first Baptist international missionary from the United States

when the believer symbolically dies and is then raised to life in the newness of Christ's grace and His call to obedience.

Baptists also see baptism as the sign of entrance into the covenant community of the body of Christ. Jesus made clear that His disciples are required to profess Him publicly (see Matt. 10:32-33). Paul reinforced a public profession of faith when he defined the essence of salvation: "With the heart one believes, resulting in righteousness, and with the mouth one confesses, resulting in salvation" (Rom. 10:10). But this public profession is not merely a public statement of belief in Christ or a public commitment to follow Christ in discipleship. It includes baptism, which represents not only the profession of the believer's faith in Christ but also the believer's commitment to enter the covenant community of the congregation and to accept all the responsibilities Christ has given believers, individually and corporately.

J. B. Gambrell (1841–1921), a plainspoken, well-known leader among Baptists a century ago, served four terms as the president of the Southern Baptist Convention. He described the symbolism involved in baptism: "Baptism is both a separating and a unifying ordinance. Symbolically it separates from the old life and commits the baptized to the new life in Christ. Therefore, we are said to put on Christ by baptism. As a common uniform unifies an army, because the uniform is a symbol of obedience and service in the one army and under one flag, so does baptism separate from the old life symbolically and bring together those who are enlisted in Christ's army. It is, therefore, a striking teaching ordinance."[4]

Baptism demonstrates a believer's obedience. Although baptism is not necessary for salvation (consider the thief on the cross), it is necessary for obedience. No believers in the New Testament resisted baptism or neglected the opportunity to obey Christ in this way.

Baptists rightly reject the notion that baptism regenerates an individual. The unbiblical concept of baptismal regeneration distorts baptism and undermines the gospel. Regeneration is God's gift that precedes baptism. Baptists do not baptize persons so that, through baptism, they can be made new creatures in Christ. Instead, we baptize persons who have already given credible evidence of salvation. Any teaching that asserts a regenerating role for baptism violates the clear New Testament teaching that we are justified by faith alone, not by faith plus anything else, including baptism (see Eph. 2:8-9).

A biblical view of baptism requires that we affirm its proper mode and its proper message. The New Testament never suggests the baptism of anyone who is not a conscious believer in the Lord Jesus Christ. Therefore, we reject the baptism of infants and anyone else who cannot consciously and personally profess faith in Christ.

Baptism is so essential to Baptists' understanding of the church (after all, it is how we got our name) that we consider it a prerequisite to other rights and responsibilities in the church, including participation in the Lord's Supper.

Baptists reject infant baptism because (choose one)—
- ☐ Scripture reserves baptism for persons who are conscious believers in Christ;
- ☐ early church history does not support infant baptism;
- ☐ baptism is commanded for adults only.

Baptists reject the belief of some groups that baptism saves (baptismal regeneration) because (choose one)—
- ☐ early Baptists voted to reject baptismal regeneration;
- ☐ the early church taught against baptismal regeneration;
- ☐ we are saved by faith alone.

Baptists look to Holy Scripture for our beliefs about the qualifications for baptism. Therefore, we must reject infant baptism because Scripture reserves baptism for persons who are conscious believers in Christ. We reject baptismal regeneration because Scripture teaches that we are saved by faith alone.

Scripture reserves baptism for persons who are conscious believers in Christ.

The Lord's Supper

The Lord's Supper, instituted by Christ Himself, points back to the Last Supper, which Christ shared with His disciples just before His crucifixion. At that meal Christ explained His atoning death in terms of bread and wine. The bread, Christ said, symbolizes His body, broken for believers. This theme is deeply rooted in Old Testament passages like the Suffering Servant texts in Isaiah (see Isa. 42; 44; 53). The broken bread points to what Christ accomplished through His active and passive obedience on the cross. His body was literally broken for us. The fruit of the vine, Jesus said, represents His blood. The theme of blood atonement runs throughout Scripture. The Bible asserts that without the shedding of blood, there is no remission of sins (see Heb. 9:22). The Book of Hebrews tells us that Jesus, our Great High Priest, once and for all entered the heavenly tabernacle and the holy of holies, not by the blood of an animal but by shedding His own blood.

Some people today find the idea of blood atonement offensive and crude, but this is the offense of the gospel. There is no way to affirm the good news of Jesus Christ without affirming blood atonement. Therefore, when Christ spoke to His disciples and said, "This cup is the new covenant established by My blood" (Luke 22:20), this was the very picture of what Christ accomplished on the cross—the very core of our salvation.

The Lord's Supper is not merely a memorial to be received by Christians. It is a congregational act in which the covenant community, in obedience to God's command and united in one faith, one Lord, and one baptism (see Eph. 4:5), obeys Christ by memorializing His sacrifice (see Luke 22:19). The Lord's Supper is not a simple reenactment of the Last Supper. It is a postresurrection celebration and commemoration of the completed work of Christ.

The scriptural command that believers examine their lives before participating in the Lord's Supper alerts believers to be on guard against persistent personal sin. Thus, carefully observing the Lord's Supper is part of the process of church discipline (see 1 Cor. 11:27-32).

Like baptism, the Lord's Supper is to be understood in symbolic terms. Baptists believe the Lord's Supper is not a sacrament but an ordinance. We do not believe the bread is literally transformed into Christ's body or the fruit of the vine is transformed into Christ's blood. Instead, we understand these elements to symbolize Christ's atoning work. Baptists believe Christ is present in His redeemed people, not in the elements of the Lord's Supper.

"Do this in remembrance of Me."
Luke 22:19

98

Mark each statement *T* (true) or *F* (false).

___ 1. The Lord's Supper is a reenactment of the Last Supper that Christ observed with His disciples.

___ 2. The Lord's Supper was instituted by the early church.

___ 3. In the Lord's Supper the bread represents the body of a believer who is wholly consecrated to God.

___ 4. The fruit of the vine represents the blood of Christ.

___ 5. The Lord's Supper helps save a person.

___ 6. The Lord's Supper alerts a believer to be on guard against personal sin.

___ 7. The elements of the Lord's Supper (bread and fruit of the vine) symbolize Christ's atoning work.

___ 8. The Lord's Supper is an ordinance for the congregation to observe together.

Statements 1, 2, 3, and 5 are false. Statements 4, 6, 7, and 8 are true.

When the local church celebrates the Lord's Supper, we proclaim the death and the resurrection of the Lord Jesus Christ even as we anticipate His return, when the church will celebrate the wedding supper of the Lamb (see Rev. 19:7). Likewise, when the church celebrates baptism, we complete the picture Christ provided for us of a believer transformed by God's grace and power. Observed regularly, baptism and the Lord's Supper teach the congregation the basic truths of our gospel. Taken together, these two ordinances not only fulfill the Lord's command but also serve as beautiful public testimonies to the sum and substance of the gospel. Believers should find great joy and satisfaction in observing and participating in these ordinances.

> "Let us be glad, rejoice, and give Him glory, because the marriage of the Lamb has come, and His wife has prepared herself."
> Revelation 19:7

Read *The Baptist Faith and Message* article on baptism and the Lord's Supper, page 93. Then complete the information called for on the following page.

The sentence that refers to baptism as a trinitarian act:

_____

Three things baptism pictures about Christ:

_____

_____

Three things baptism pictures about the person being baptized:

_____

_____

The word that refers to the mode of baptism: _____

The word that identifies the person being baptized:

_____

The statement that speaks of the relationship of baptism to church membership:

_____

The two things church members do by taking part in the Lord's Supper.

_____

Think about your baptism and Lord's Supper observances you have experienced. Thank Christ for the two memorials He left us.

CHAPTER 11

THE LORD'S DAY

Article 8

The Lord's Day

"The first day of the week is the Lord's Day. It is a Christian institution for regular observance. It commemorates the resurrection of Christ from the dead and should include exercises of worship and spiritual devotion, both public and private. Activities on the Lord's Day should be commensurate with the Christian's conscience under the Lordship of Jesus Christ."[1]

Memory Verse

"I rejoiced with those who said to me,

'Let us go to the house of the LORD.'" Psalm 122:1

Christians gather together and celebrate worship on the Lord's Day. This practice is deeply rooted in the Christian tradition and in the practice of Christian churches from the time of the apostles. Sunday is not arbitrarily chosen as the Lord's Day but is designated as such in Scripture, which states that the apostles and other disciples gathered for worship on the first day of the week (see Acts 20:7). Without doubt, this practice is tied to the resurrection of the Lord Jesus Christ on the first day of the week, indicating the centrality of resurrection faith to the very structure of the church in Christian worship.

Regular Observance

The Baptist Faith and Message identifies the Lord's Day as "a Christian institution for regular observance." Of course, because the Lord's Day is identified with the first day of the week, that regular observance translates into a weekly event. In the rhythm of life, Christians gather on the first day of the week, and this regular observance gives structure to Christian commitment and discipleship.

> The Lord's Day is the day by which all other days are judged.

In a very real sense, the Lord's Day is the day by which all other days are judged. The Lord's Day is the one day when we affirm that Christians are to give priority not only to acts of personal devotion and discipleship in obedience to Christ but also to corporate worship. The Lord Jesus Christ commissioned His church to be in the world—and so we are during the week. Believers are to be actively involved in the affairs of the world—in commerce, in politics, in every sphere of life—as salt and light (see Matt. 5:13). But the gathered community of the church is called together on the Lord's Day to fulfill the biblical command that we not forsake the assembling of ourselves together: "Let us be concerned about one another in order to promote love and good works, not staying away from our meetings, as some habitually do, but encouraging each other, and all the more as you see the day drawing near" (Heb. 10:25).

The First Day of the Week

Christians have sometimes argued over the appropriate day for worship. There is no question that the Sabbath command, as revealed in the Ten Commandments, focused on the seventh day of the week—the day we now know as Saturday. Thus, the Jewish people have considered Saturday as the Sabbath from Old Testament times. This raises a very important distinction and a crucial question for the church: is the Lord's Day the Sabbath? This has been an issue of heated Christian controversy. Some groups, such as Seventh-Day Adventists and Seventh-Day Baptists, believe Christians should gather on the last day of the week—Saturday—in order to fulfill the Old Testament command. In their view the church should simply follow the pattern and practice of the Jewish people.

This understanding of the Lord's Day raises at least two problems. The first is biblical. We have ample reason to believe that the earliest Christians shifted their day of observance from Saturday to Sunday because Christ appeared to His disciples on the first day of the week. John 20:19 reveals that on the first day of the week—the Sunday after the crucifixion—Christ appeared to His disciples and revealed His wounded hands and side. The disciples' rejoicing that Jesus had risen from the dead is a hallmark of true Christian worship. The Sunday observance of the Lord's Day certainly points to the centrality of the resurrection to the Christian faith, affirming what the Apostle Paul wrote to the Corinthians—that he delivered to them what was the first priority:

> ... that Christ died for our sins according
>   to the Scriptures,
> that He was buried,
> that He was raised on the third day
>   according to the Scriptures.
> 1 Corinthians 15:3-4

The second problem with interpreting the Lord's Day as Saturday is the practice and tradition of the church. Acts 20:7 tells us that the believers came together "on the first day of the week" for the breaking of bread and for preaching, a clear reference to corporate worship. It is absolutely clear that from the earliest days of the church, Christians gathered on Sunday rather than on Saturday.

The Sunday observance of the Lord's Day certainly points to the centrality of the resurrection to the Christian faith.

Fill in the blanks to contrast the Lord's Day with the Sabbath.

The Sabbath	*The Lord's Day*
Observed by Jews	Observed by _____
The seventh day of the week	The _____ day of the week
Commemorates God's creative work and His resting on the seventh day	Commemorates _____ _____ _____
Emphasis on abstaining from work	Emphasis on _____ _____

Check the two reasons Christians observe Sunday as the day for Christian worship rather than Saturday, the Jewish Sabbath.

☐ 1. The early church wanted to depart from the Old Testament command to observe the Sabbath.

☐ 2. Christ appeared to His disciples on Sunday following His resurrection.

☐ 3. The Sunday observance of the Lord's Day points to the certainty of Christ's return.

☐ 4. The early believers gathered for corporate worship on Sunday rather than on Saturday.

☐ 5. Christ commanded His disciples to observe Sunday as the Lord's Day.

You should have checked statements 2 and 4.

Worship and Spiritual Devotion

The purpose of gathering on the Lord's Day is, as *The Baptist Faith and Message* says, for "exercises of worship and spiritual devotion, both public and private." Sensitive and difficult questions relate to what Christians should and should not do on the Lord's Day, and Christians sometimes disagree. Some argue that obedience to the Fourth Commandment requires that Christians avoid any labor or entertainment on the Lord's Day. Others argue that the Fourth Commandment

Sensitive and difficult questions relate to what Christians should and should not do on the Lord's Day.

has been fulfilled in Christ and does not lay a burden on Christians about entertainment, necessary work, and other activities as long as time, priority, and full attention are given to the church gathered for worship.

This debate goes all the way back to the time of the apostles (see Rom. 14:5-6). The Jewish authorities had turned the Sabbath into a burden for God's people. Rabbis were involved in pointless debates over what could and could not be done on the Sabbath. Jesus rebuked this kind of thinking when He told the Pharisees, "The Sabbath was made for man, not man for the Sabbath" (Mark 2:27).

Similarly, Christians can transform the Lord's Day observance into acts of artificial legalism, thus missing the entire point of the day. The Lord's Day is one of Christ's gifts to His church. This good gift reminds us that true Christian worship is a celebration and that the Lord's Day should be a day of great joy and peace.

Christians should strive to order their lives so that they do not neglect the priority of corporate worship on the Lord's Day. Believers should find deep, uncompromised joy in such worship and should order their lives to best demonstrate that priority. The Christian's conscience, informed by Scripture, yielded to Christ's lordship, and accountable to the local congregation, must guide the believer's decision making about how to observe the Lord's Day.

> "One person considers one day to be above another day. Someone else considers every day to be the same. Each one must be fully convinced in his own mind. Whoever observes the day, observes it to the Lord. Whoever eats, eats to the Lord, since he gives thanks to God; and whoever does not eat, it is to the Lord that he does not eat, yet he thanks God."
> Romans 14:5-6

Concerning work and entertainment on the Lord's Day, Christians should be guided by (choose one)—

☐ the church;
☐ their conscience;
☐ the practice of other Christians;
☐ the community.

A Christian's primary activity on the Lord's Day should be

_____.

Corporate worship is at the very center of Christian devotion. Christians gather to proclaim the majesty and glory of God and to proclaim the gospel. In the context of worship, believers are confronted and fed

"Let the message about the Messiah dwell richly among you, teaching and admonishing one another in all wisdom, and singing psalms, hymns, and spiritual songs, with gratitude in your hearts to God."

Colossians 3:16

by the preaching of God's Word and jointly confess the faith through songs and hymns, Scripture reading, and prayer (see Col. 3:16). At the same time, Scripture encourages Christians to engage in private acts of devotion, such as Scripture reading and prayer, and in acts of Christian service (see 2 Cor. 8:1-3; 1 Thess. 5:12,17; 2 Tim. 3:16; Jas. 1:27). Of course, these acts of personal devotion are a Christian's responsibility every day of the week, but the Lord's Day offers a unique opportunity for a serious, thankful response to what the believer has experienced in the context of corporate worship.

Check the four main elements of corporate worship.
- ☐ Songs and hymns
- ☐ Ministry to the sick
- ☐ Prayer
- ☐ Evangelistic visitation
- ☐ Scripture reading
- ☐ Preaching
- ☐ Drama

Check the three main elements of private devotion.
- ☐ Scripture reading
- ☐ Preaching
- ☐ Acts of Christian service
- ☐ Songs and hymns
- ☐ Prayer

If a neighbor asked you, "Why do you work on Saturday and worship on Sunday? You're breaking one of the Ten Commandments," how would you respond?

_____

_____

Close your study of this chapter by reading aloud Psalm 63 as a prayer from your heart to God.

106

CHAPTER 12

THE KINGDOM

Article 9

The Kingdom

"The Kingdom of God includes both His general sovereignty over the universe and His particular kingship over men who willfully acknowledge Him as King. Particularly the Kingdom is the realm of salvation into which men enter by trustful, childlike commitment to Jesus Christ. Christians ought to pray and to labor that the Kingdom may come and God's will be done on earth. The full consummation of the Kingdom awaits the return of Jesus Christ and the end of this age."[1]

> **Memory Verse**
>
> "Seek first the kingdom of God and His righteousness,
>
> and all these things will be provided for you."
>
> Matthew 6:33

Kingdom of God

God's sovereign rule in the universe and in the hearts of Christians

The true and living God is King, and His kingdom represents His rule and His power. The Bible is filled with images and metaphors of royalty. When Isaiah saw the Lord in his vision recorded in Isaiah 6:1-8, he saw the Lord "seated on a high and lofty throne, and His robe filled the temple" (v. 1). God is the great heavenly King.

Read *The Baptist Faith and Message* article on the kingdom, page 107. List the two areas of sovereignty included in the kingdom of God.

1. _____

2. _____

"When the Son of Man comes in His glory, and all the angels with Him, then He will sit on the throne of His glory."
Matthew 25:31

How can a person can enter the kingdom of God?

_____

When will the full consummation of the kingdom take place?

_____

"A child will be born for us, a son will be given to us, and the government will be on His shoulders. He will be named Wonderful Counselor, Mighty God, Eternal Father, Prince of Peace."
Isaiah 9:6

The Bible also uses royal imagery to refer to Christ. Jesus told His disciples to look for Him to return and sit on a glorious throne (see Matt. 25:31). Jesus is the Prince of Peace, the Alpha and Omega who sits on the throne of His kingdom (see Isa. 9:6; Rev. 21:5-6).

The kingdom of God is not like the kingdoms of this world. Earthly kingdoms are temporary; the kingdom of God is eternal. Earthly kings rule over finite kingdoms, but God's rule knows no limitations. The power of an earthly monarch is limited by his partial sovereignty, but God's rule is established in His unconditional and supreme sovereignty. Thus, the kingdom of God is an unshakable kingdom—a kingdom in which God's rule is so absolute and so perfect that His creatures live only to please, obey, and glorify Him (see Heb. 12:28).

Refer to the previous paragraph as you contrast earthly kingdoms with God's kingdom.

Earthly Kingdoms	*God's Kingdom*
Temporary	_____
Finite	_____
Limited power	_____
Sinful by nature	_____

The Kingdom in Scripture

The kingdom of God is a major theme throughout the Bible. Scripture presents us with an understanding of the kingdom that is deeply rooted in biblical history, very relevant to the present, but ultimately focused on the future.

In the Old Testament the kingdom of God is seen in God's rule over all His creation. God is pictured as a King whose sovereignty extends to the ends of the earth, encompassing all of the cosmos (see Ps. 47:2,7; 95:3). God is behind the rise and the fall of nations (see 2 Chron. 20:6; Job 12:23; Ps. 22:28). His kingly rule is both benevolent and deeply rooted in justice (see Ps. 99:4).

The Old Testament writers understood that God's purposes would be worked out in the unfolding of human history. At the same time, the Old Testament picture of the kingdom of God was incomplete, pointing to what would be fulfilled in the New Testament.

In the New Testament Jesus frequently preached about the kingdom of God—even as He announced His own ministry—and declared that the kingdom of God was at hand (see Matt. 4:17). In other words, where Christ is present, the kingdom of God is present. Clearly, this statement was in an anticipatory form, for when Christ's kingdom is fully realized,

> Every knee should bow …
> and every tongue should confess
> that Jesus Christ is Lord,
> to the glory of God the Father.
> Philippians 2:10-11

"The One seated on the throne said, 'Look! I am making everything new.' He also said, 'Write, because these words are faithful and true.' And He said to me, 'It is done! I am the Alpha and the Omega, the Beginning and the End. I will give to the thirsty from the spring of living water as a gift.' "
Revelation 21:5-6

"Since we are receiving a kingdom that cannot be shaken, let us hold on to grace. By it, we may serve God acceptably, with reverence and awe."
Hebrews 12:28

Christ's appearing as the sign that the kingdom of God had come was evident in His miracles, in the fact that demons obeyed His command, and in the fact that even the wind and waves obeyed His voice.

Check three outward signs that the kingdom of God arrived when Jesus came to earth.
- ☐ He performed miracles.
- ☐ He told parables.
- ☐ The elements of nature obeyed Him.
- ☐ Demons obeyed Him.
- ☐ The disciples followed Him.
- ☐ The crowds gathered to hear Him.

The truth of God's sovereignty is absolutely central to the Bible's presentation of the kingdom of God. Most of us understand the concept of a monarchy, in which a king exercises absolute rule over his kingdom. This is precisely the picture the Bible presents for our understanding of God's rule over all creation. Although human leaders are limited in power and are sinful by nature, God rules His kingdom with absolutely unlimited sovereignty, completely unconstrained power, and absolute justice that reflects His holiness.

God rules His kingdom with absolutely unlimited sovereignty, completely unconstrained power, and absolute justice that reflects His holiness.

Read each Scripture and match the reference with the correct summary statement.

___ 1. Isaiah 9:6-7   a. The new birth is essential to enter the kingdom.

___ 2. Matthew 6:33   b. The kingdom of God begins small but grows.

___ 3. Matthew 13:3-9   c. People who have entered the kingdom and those who have not must coexist.

___ 4. Matthew 13:24-30   d. The Son's kingdom will be established forever.

___ 5. Matthew 13:31-32   e. Jesus will fellowship with His people in His kingdom.

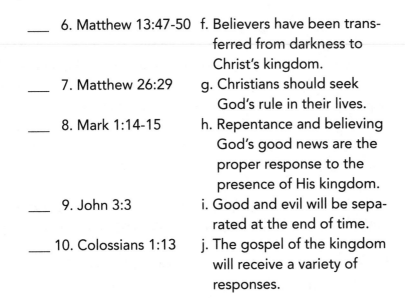

___ 6. Matthew 13:47-50   f. Believers have been trans-
ferred from darkness to
Christ's kingdom.

___ 7. Matthew 26:29   g. Christians should seek
God's rule in their lives.

___ 8. Mark 1:14-15   h. Repentance and believing
God's good news are the
proper response to the
presence of His kingdom.

___ 9. John 3:3   i. Good and evil will be separated at the end of time.

___ 10. Colossians 1:13   j. The gospel of the kingdom
will receive a variety of
responses.

How did you match the verses? We matched them this way: 1. d, 2. g, 3. j, 4. c, 5. b, 6. i, 7. e, 8. h, 9. a, 10. f.

The Kingdom and the Church

Although God's rule extends to all people in all places and at all times, the kingdom of God is identified with and understood by those who confess Jesus Christ as Lord. Christians have experienced the arrival of the kingdom of God in the person and work of Jesus Christ. They have submitted themselves to His authority over their lives, their behavior, and their possessions. In other words, everything in a believer's life is under Jesus' authority. Thus, those who have experienced the new birth and have joined the body of Christ understand that the kingdom of God is present in their personal lives and in the church, but they also know that God's kingdom will ultimately be realized at the end of time, when Christ reigns over the entire cosmos.

> Christians have experienced the arrival of the kingdom of God in the person and work of Jesus Christ.

We must be careful not to make an absolute identification between the church and the kingdom. The church is the eternal people of God, whereas the kingdom is the eternal rule of God. God's kingdom extends beyond the church, even throughout the new heaven and the new earth and to all orders of created beings, including angels.

However, in this age and on this planet, the church is the visible representation of the kingdom of God in all its power and promises. Jesus instructed His disciples to pray, "Your kingdom come" (Matt. 6:10). Such a prayer is an important act of Christian discipleship that represents not only confidence in God's eventual rule but also determination to faithfully represent God's kingdom in our lives. Ultimately, the revelation of the kingdom of God awaits the return of Jesus Christ and the total consummation of God's purposes.

> Ultimately, the revelation of the kingdom of God awaits the return of Jesus Christ.

In the previous paragraph underline the two things represented when a Christian prays, "Your kingdom come."

A person can enter the kingdom of God by—
☐ observing the Golden Rule;
☐ trusting Jesus Christ as Savior and Lord;
☐ joining a church;
☐ keeping the Ten Commandments.

Evaluate the degree to which the following areas of your life are under Jesus' authority.

	Not much			Very much	
Your thought life	1	2	3	4	5
The books you read	1	2	3	4	5
Your hobbies and recreation	1	2	3	4	5
Your use of the computer	1	2	3	4	5
Your music and entertainment	1	2	3	4	5

What is one way you can more faithfully represent the kingdom of God in your life?

_____

Close your study of this chapter by studying the prayer in Matthew 6:9-13 and then praying the prayer. Ask God to help you represent His kingdom in every area of your life.

CHAPTER 13

LAST THINGS

Article 10

Last Things

"God, in His own time and in His own way, will bring the world to its appropriate end. According to His promise, Jesus Christ will return personally and visibly in glory to the earth; the dead will be raised; and Christ will judge all men in righteousness. The unrighteous will be consigned to Hell, the place of everlasting punishment. The righteous in their resurrected and glorified bodies will receive their reward and will dwell forever in Heaven with the Lord."[1]

Memory Verses

"Your heart must not be troubled. Believe in God; believe also in Me. In My Father's house are many dwelling places; if not, I would have told you. I am going away to prepare a place for you. If I go away and prepare a place for you, I will come back and receive you to Myself, so that where I am you may be also." John 14:1-3

Eschatology
The study of Last Things or the end time, when Christ will return

The Bible depicts a timeline that includes past, present, and future. God is not trapped in or limited by time. He created time as a construct within eternity—part of His creation. From the very beginning, time was to be limited in duration. Our experience as human beings is inextricably linked to time. We cannot imagine life without it, but we are promised a day when time will be no more. While the Bible points us to the past for an understanding of God's work and the unfolding of His plan in history and while the Bible takes the present very seriously, it also places a central focus on things to come.

The Bible's doctrine of eschatology, which focuses on Last Things, provides a future horizon for Christian theology and Christian living. Believers are to live in anticipation of Christ's coming and in absolute confidence that God will consummate all things and accomplish His purposes.

Read *The Baptist Faith and Message* article on Last Things, page 113.

"I will create a new heaven and a new earth; the past events will not be remembered or come to mind."
Isaiah 65:17

When the world will end? _____

Describe the manner in which Christ will return to earth.

_____

"I saw a new heaven and a new earth, for the first heaven and the first earth had passed away, and the sea existed no longer."
Revelation 21:1

List four things that will take place when Christ returns.
1. _____
2. _____
3. _____
4. _____

For Christians, while the world is a place of incredible beauty and wonder, it is also a place of grave danger. We understand that creation is fallen, as revealed in Scripture. But even as we live and witness in this fallen world, we look forward to a new heaven and a new earth (see Isa. 65:17; Rev. 21:1). This world will come to a necessary end.

As *The Baptist Faith and Message* states, "God, in His own time and in His own way, will bring the world to its appropriate end." This knowledge should humble and comfort believers.

Believers differ on the details related to Last Things. Herschel Hobbs wrote, "Since the New Testament speaks in broad terms about last things, it is to be expected that problems would arise as to the interpretation of details. For instance, interpreters differ as to the number of comings, resurrections, judgments, and the millennium, along with certain other details as to the end of the age. ... It is sufficient to say that one's position as to details has never been a test of orthodoxy among Baptists."[2]

Read each Scripture and match the reference with the correct summary statement.

___ 1. Matthew 24:36	a. Jesus will return when people do not expect Him.
___ 2. Matthew 24:37-44	
___ 3. Luke 12:8-9	b. Jesus will return with power and glory.
___ 4. Luke 21:27	
___ 5. John 5:28-29	c. Everyone will stand before God in judgment.
___ 6. Acts 1:11	
___ 7. Revelation 20:11-13	d. No one knows when Jesus will return.
	e. Jesus will return as He went away.
	f. Someone's eternal destiny is decided in this life.
	g. Death is not the end of people.

You probably answered 1. d, 2. a, 3. f, 4. b, 5. g, 6. e, 7. c.

The Return of Christ

The doctrine of Last Things focuses especially on Jesus Christ and His return. The Bible tells us that He will return to earth personally, visibly, and gloriously. Christ's coming, often referred to as the Lord's second coming, will be quite different from His birth. In Bethlehem

Jesus will return to earth personally, visibly, and gloriously.

He entered human existence in the form of a lowly baby. His first place of residence was an animal's humble feeding trough. There were no trappings of majesty, and the shepherds saw God's glory displayed in the weakness of a baby (see Luke 2:1-16).

When Christ returns, however, He will come in glory as a conquering king to claim His kingdom. Christ will return visibly so that all creatures will see Him, as the natural world testified of Christ's finished work when the earth trembled and the clouds darkened at Calvary (see Matt. 27:45,51). When Christ returns, He will come in the clouds, the heavens parting to signal his arrival (see Luke 21:27; 1 Thess. 4:17).

David Dockery (1952–), a leading Southern Baptist theologian and the president of Union University in Jackson, Tennessee, wrote, "The reality of Christ's return is grounded in the overall purposes of God. The central themes of the Christian message accompanying the proclamation of Jesus' lordship include His sinlessness, death, resurrection, ascension, and His return. These assurances brought hope to the early church as they do to us today. From the beginning, the climactic event of Christ's return has been at the heart of Christian preaching, echoing the words of Jesus Himself: 'And then they will see the Son of Man coming in clouds with great power and glory' (Mark 13:26). Wherever the apostles preached, they preached the reality of this announcement."[3]

> "They will see the Son of Man coming in a cloud with power and great glory."
> Luke 21:27

> "We who are still alive will be caught up together with them in the clouds to meet the Lord in the air; and so we will always be with the Lord."
> 1 Thessalonians 4:17

Name two ways Christ's return will differ from His first coming.

1. _____

2. _____

How does the promise of His return give you hope?

_____

_____

The Resurrection of the Dead

When Christ returns, the dead will be raised (see 1 Thess. 4:16). The promise of our resurrection is sure and certain. All those who have died—believers and unbelievers—will experience the resurrection of the dead. The Apostle Paul assured believers that we will be resurrected because of Christ's resurrection: "Since death came through a man, the resurrection of the dead also comes through a man. For just as in Adam all die, so also in Christ all will be made alive" (1 Cor. 15:21-22).

What guarantee do believers have that we will be resurrected?

_____

> "The Lord Himself will descend from heaven with a shout, with the archangel's voice, and with the trumpet of God, and the dead in Christ will rise first."
>
> 1 Thessalonians 4:16

Christ's resurrection guarantees our own. Our resurrection precedes the judgment that is to come. On this day of judgment, God will judge all human beings, and Christ will judge all people in righteousness. The righteous—those who are declared righteous through faith in Christ—will be allowed into heaven. The unrighteous will be consigned to hell, the place of everlasting punishment (see Rev. 20:11-15).

Eternal Destiny

Polls indicate that the vast majority of Americans not only believe in heaven and hell but also believe they will certainly go to heaven. The popular conception of heaven is that it is a place of unlimited leisure and sensual or trivial enjoyment. Furthermore, most Americans believe they will be there because they think themselves at least as good as their neighbors, and they see no reason God should not welcome them into heaven. Completely missing from this popular conception is the Bible's insistence that heaven is God's gift only to those who are redeemed in Christ. Heaven is the eternal dwelling place of believers in the presence of God and in the company of the saints (see John 14:2-3; Phil. 3:20).

We can anticipate heaven as a state of existence and a place where believers, now both resurrected and glorified, will serve, praise, and honor God forever. The picture found in the Book of Revelation helps us understand what we will do in heaven. Our task will be to declare God's glory and to exult in His holiness forever, joining the angels and the other heavenly beings in enjoying the infinite pleasure of being in the presence of Almighty God (see Rev. 4:8,11). Thus, the church lives in anticipation of Christ's coming and prays, "Come, Lord Jesus" (Rev. 22:20).

Check the things believers will likely do in heaven.
- ☐ 1. Enjoy sensual pleasures
- ☐ 2. Serve God
- ☐ 3. Praise God
- ☐ 4. Float on a cloud
- ☐ 5. Enjoy God's presence

You probably checked 2, 3, and 5.

In contrast to heaven, hell is the place of eternal judgment, punishment, and torment. The Bible's presentation of hell is straightforward and honest. Indeed, more verses speak directly of hell than of heaven. Jesus warned that we should not so much fear the one who can destroy the body but the one who can destroy both body and soul in hell (see Matt. 10:28).

The Bible's portrayal of this doctrine centers on hell's nature as a place of eternal, conscious torment. This is made clear in Luke 16, in the narrative about Lazarus and the rich man. This passage tells us much about the future, pointing to the eternal distinction between those in God's presence and those excluded from God's presence forever. But hell is not merely a place where God's presence is absent. It is a place where God's judgment is manifested in the conscious torment and suffering of those who have refused God's grace, broken God's law, and received God's just punishment for their sins.

The New Testament picture of hell uses such powerful and awful images as fire and brimstone (see Matt. 3:10; 5:22; Mark 9:48; Jas. 3:6; 2 Pet. 3:7; Jude 1:7; Rev. 20:14). These comparisons should cause all of us to take hell with great seriousness. Nevertheless, in recent years some theologians have attempted to dispense with hell. In modern

> "Holy, holy, holy, Lord God, the Almighty, who was, who is, and who is coming. Our Lord and God, You are worthy to receive glory and honor and power, because You have created all things, and because of Your will they exist and were created."
> Revelation 4:8,11

times hell has become politically incorrect and particularly offensive to the postmodern mind. Christians must understand that hell is clearly revealed in the Bible. Furthermore, we must understand that the biblical passages about hell serve as warnings both to believers and to unbelievers. For believers the warnings should serve as an impetus to evangelism and as a constant reminder of what is at stake in the distinction between belief and unbelief. For unbelievers hell should serve as a clear and present warning that if they do not come to faith in Christ and if their sins remain unforgiven, they will bear the full weight of God's wrath poured out on their sin.

The Final Judgment

The final judgment, as taught in Scripture, provides an essential frame of reference for the Christian life. Believers need to know that God's justice will be fully realized. In this life we understand that all attempts at justice are finite and fallible. We must also understand that even when we see God's judgment being revealed in our own times, we must anticipate the absolute, ultimate, and final display of God's justice and holiness on the day of judgment. We need this frame of final judgment and the promise of consummation to understand our times. We are to live in anticipation of God's total consummation of His purposes and the final, comprehensive display of His glory.

The Bible refers to this expectation as "the blessed hope" (Titus 2:13). Believers must live and work in light of this sure and certain hope. This is another sobering reminder that we will face God's judgment. For believers this judgment is secure and safe because of the work of Christ (see 1 John 4:17). Scripture promises that Christ will claim His own and that on the day of judgment believers will find in Christ an advocate who will ensure our salvation (see Rom. 5:1; 1 John 2:1). On that day God will not accept believers on the basis of anything we have done, but He will declare our sins forgiven in Christ.

Name two ways God's judgment represents a blessed hope for believers.

1. _____

2. _____

"Love is perfected with us so that we may have confidence in the day of judgment."
1 John 4:17

"Since we have been declared righteous by faith, we have peace with God through our Lord Jesus Christ."
Romans 5:1

We have many reasons to hope in God's judgment. At that time God will bring about justice, we will understand God's activity and purposes during our lives, and we will see God's glory displayed. We will be secure at that time because Jesus' righteousness covers our sin.

> **Believers will receive rewards commensurate with Christian devotion and service.**

Believers will also face judgment for our deeds in terms of obedience and disobedience to God's commands. The Bible reveals that believers, having been resurrected and glorified, will receive rewards commensurate with Christian devotion and service (see Matt. 16:27; Luke 6:35; 14:13-14; Gal. 6:9). The Bible does not specifically tell us how to understand these rewards, but we are to anticipate God's judgment, knowing that God's determination will be absolutely perfect and righteous.

Mark each statement _T_ (true) or _F_ (false) to review your study of Last Things.

___ 1. God is not bound by time.

___ 2. Christ will return in humility.

___ 3. The dead will be resurrected when Christ returns.

___ 4. Heaven is a place where we will serve and praise God.

___ 5. Scripture uses images to describe hell to indicate that hell is a symbol of judgment, not a real place.

___ 6. At the final judgment believers will be declared righteous in Christ.

You should have answered 1. T, 2. F, 3. T, 4. T, 5. F, 6. T.

If you knew that Jesus would return in a few days, what changes would you make in your life?

_____

_____

Thank God that He holds the future. Ask Him to help you live more expectantly for Christ's second coming.

120

CHAPTER 14

EVANGELISM AND MISSIONS

Article 11

Evangelism and Missions

"It is the duty and privilege of every follower of Christ and of every church of the Lord Jesus Christ to endeavor to make disciples of all nations. The new birth of man's spirit by God's Holy Spirit means the birth of love for others. Missionary effort on the part of all rests thus upon a spiritual necessity of the regenerate life, and is expressly and repeatedly commanded in the teachings of Christ. The Lord Jesus Christ has commanded the preaching of the gospel to all nations. It is the duty of every child of God to seek constantly to win the lost to Christ by verbal witness undergirded by a Christian lifestyle, and by other methods in harmony with the gospel of Christ."[1]

> **Memory Verses**
>
> " 'Everyone who calls on the name of the Lord will be saved.' But how can they call on Him in whom they have not believed? And how can they believe without hearing about Him? And how can they hear without a preacher? And how can they preach unless they are sent? As it is written: 'How welcome are the feet of those who announce the gospel of good things!' " Romans 10:13-15

"Go, therefore, and make disciples of all nations, baptizing them in the name of the Father and of the Son and of the Holy Spirit, teaching them to observe everything I have commanded you. And remember, I am with you always, to the end of the age."

Matthew 28:19-20

Evangelism
The central component of the church's mission, which involves telling others the gospel of salvation with the goal of leading them to repentance and faith in Christ

Evangelism is one of the church's central responsibilities. Christ's final command to the church, known as the Great Commission (see Matt. 28:19-20), makes this priority clear. Our Lord instructed the church to make disciples of all nations, baptizing them in the name of the Father, the Son, and the Holy Spirit.

Read the Great Commission in Matthew 28:19-20.

The main command in verse 19 is to make _____.
The next step after a person professes faith in Christ
is _____. The church has the responsibility to
_____ new converts. Christians can be assured
of the presence of _____ to the end of the age.

The Baptist Faith and Message states, "It is the duty and privilege of every follower of Christ and of every church of the Lord Jesus Christ to endeavor to make disciples of all nations." Lee Scarborough emphasized the responsibility of every Christian to witness for Christ: "The divine obligation of soul-winning rests without exception upon every child of God. The Christian receives the essence of this obligation and call at the time of his salvation. ... The fruit of a Christian is another Christian."[2] Scarborough also emphasized the importance of sharing the gospel throughout the world: "At any cost we are to go into all the world and to all individuals of every nation, to every creature, and give this gospel."[3]

Duty and Privilege

The biblical roots of evangelism are deep. The church understands its responsibility in evangelism as the fulfillment of God's redemptive purpose. Evangelism is not merely a program; it is an assignment Christ invested in His church. Our task is to be heralds and witnesses of what Christ has done for us so that others might also come to a saving knowledge of Jesus Christ.

Throughout its history the church has regarded evangelism as a central responsibility and an act of Christian love. Unfortunately, in some eras the church has conceived of evangelism in terms other than direct witness to individuals. Biblical Christians do not believe in evangelism by the sword, by coercion, by baptism, or by any means other than sharing the gospel and allowing sinners to respond freely to the grace of the Lord Jesus Christ.

Today opposition to evangelism can come from a variety of sources. Theological liberalism has abandoned any understanding of divine judgment and any threat of hell. Thus, evangelism is often transformed into social liberation or another form of social activism. We must resist the charge that Christians who share the gospel are engaging in cultural imperialism or religious bigotry. The Lord Jesus made clear that He is the Way, the Truth, and the Life. He continued, "No one comes to the Father except through Me" (John 14:6). The disciples affirmed this truth, declaring, "There is salvation in no one else, for there is no other name under heaven given to people by which we must be saved" (Acts 4:12). The exclusivity of the gospel is a nonnegotiable Christian truth that is deeply grounded in Scripture and is essential to our understanding of the missionary mandate and its priority.

Others suggest that evangelism need not take the form of direct verbal witness to the Lord Jesus Christ. No one in the New Testament came to a saving knowledge of Jesus Christ merely by observing Christians and their lifestyle. A verbal presentation of the gospel is absolutely necessary and is central to God's plan for the spread of the gospel and the expansion of the church (see Rom. 10:13-17).

Underline the set of words that correctly completes each statement.
- We have (one way, many ways) to God.
- Christians who share the gospel are (bigoted, compassionate).

To All Nations

Evangelism and missions go hand in hand, but missions has historically been understood as a means of reaching nations and people groups rather than individuals alone. The Great Commission clearly assigns both evangelism and missions to the church, with missions understood to be the strategy for taking the gospel to the ends of the earth. In our day, due to rapid advances in communications and

Missions
The church's God-given responsibility to bring God's love and the Christian gospel to all people through evangelism, education, and ministry

transportation, some of the historical barriers to missions have fallen away. At the same time, we still face the unique and demanding challenge of reaching people who speak different languages, share different cultures, and operate from different cultural contexts and worldviews. Thus, missions must always be done with respect and must be motivated by love for the peoples to be reached for Christ.

> Missions must always be done with respect and must be motivated by love for the peoples to be reached for Christ.

What are some advances in our world today that facilitate missions?

_____

What are some challenges in our world today that hinder reaching people with the gospel?

_____

Adoniram Judson served in Burma (modern Myanmar) for 38 years, returning home for furlough only one time. He endured imprisonment and torture, the loss of family members, and lifelong poor health. Judson labored for 23 years to translate the entire Bible into Burmese. He died on board a ship in the Bay of Bengal and was buried at sea.[4]

Judson's legacy continued through the decades that followed. In the early 1950s a 10-year old boy, John Cuai Sang, from the Chin tribe in Burma, professed faith in Christ. Earning a doctorate at the Asian Baptist Theological Seminary in the Philippines, Sang served in Burma for 30 years as a pastor. In 1999 he began a Christian school in Yangon with 10 students. Today the Institute of Mission and Church Planting is a thriving 4-year school that trains men and women in the Bible, evangelism, and church planting. Combining academic work with field experience, the students conduct an evangelistic emphasis every weekend in Yangon and take mission trips each year to different parts of Myanmar. Students share the gospel with around five thousand people each year. Dr. Sang died in 2006, and now the school is directed by his son, Thawng Za Lian, also a graduate of the seminary. The Bible used by the students is the one Judson translated.[5]

We are being compassionate when we share the good news. William Carey (1761–1834), who served 41 years in India without returning home to England, is known as the father of modern missions. He wrote, "The thought of a fellow creature perishing for ever should rouse all our activity and engage all our powers. ... The matter is desperate. It calls for us to live and act alone for God."[6]

Evangelical Christians understand that life and death hang in the balance and that a saving knowledge of the Lord Jesus Christ is all that separates sinners from hell. For this reason Christian evangelism and the missionary task are driven by love. As *The Baptist Faith and Message* reminds us, "The new birth of man's spirit by God's Holy Spirit means the birth of love for others." That love is best expressed in a bold, sensitive Christian witness.

The power of a Christian's verbal witness is greatly enhanced by the illustration of a believer's life and acts of service in Christ's name. Proponents of lifestyle evangelism rightly suggest that Christians are to be witnesses in the way we live, the way we work, the way we raise our children, and the way we engage others in society. Indeed, our lifestyle should point to our salvation and to God's power realized in us through the gospel. Acts of service and ministry to people in need can open doors for a gospel witness. Bill Wallace and the staff of Stout Memorial Hospital in Wuchow vividly illustrated this truth as their ministry of love and healing became known throughout south China. "Bill Wallace was a doctor; his basic ministry was one of healing. But he was in China first of all as a bearer of the good news of Jesus Christ, the glad tidings of forgiveness and eternal life inherent in the old, old message of God's love. Sometimes his soft, stuttering witness to that grace was more effective than the most eloquent evangelist's plea."[9] Wallace sealed his testimony with his life: the 43-year-old doctor was murdered by the Communists on February 10, 1951.[10]

Evangelism and missions are not for religious professionals alone. Every Christian is charged with the responsibility to share the gospel and to tell others how they can come to know Jesus Christ and receive the gift of everlasting life.

> "The steadfast love of the Lord fills this whole earth. It has laid hold on us and made us aware that we must share it with all the world.[7] With all my heart I believe Christians are responsible to give the Gospel to every person in the world."[8]
>
> Baker James Cauthen
> 1909–85
> Executive secretary, Foreign Mission Board (now International Mission Board) of the Southern Baptist Convention, 1954–79

Mark each statement and *T* (true) or *F* (false).

___ 1. Evangelism is a priority for the church.

___ 2. Evangelism should primarily emphasize practical issues like equality, discrimination, health, jobs, and housing.

___ 3. The essence of evangelism is sharing what Christ has done for us and what He can do for others.

___ 4. Christians can witness adequately through their daily lives.

___ 5. A verbal presentation of the gospel is necessary for a person to come to faith in Christ.

Read each Scripture passage. Match each reference with the correct summary statement.

___ 1. Matthew 9:37-38
___ 2. John 3:16
___ 3. John 20:21
___ 4. Acts 1:8
___ 5. Romans 10:13-15

a. God loves every person and sent Christ to save all who believe in Him.

b. Christ commanded us to go into all the world and witness.

c. Everyone who calls on Jesus will be saved, but they must first hear about Him.

d. Jesus sends us even as God sent Him.

e. A huge harvest awaits with few workers; we must pray for more workers.

Statements 1, 3, and 5 are true; statements 2 and 4 are false. You probably matched the Scriptures this way: 1. e, 2. a, 3. d, 4. b, 5. c.

Spend a few minutes reflecting on the need for every believer to be a witness for Christ. Reflect on the need to reach our lost and broken world for the Savior. Pray, renewing your commitment to witness for Christ.

CHAPTER 15

EDUCATION

Article 12
Education

"Christianity is the faith of enlightenment and intelligence. In Jesus Christ abide all the treasures of wisdom and knowledge. All sound learning is, therefore, a part of our Christian heritage. The new birth opens all human faculties and creates a thirst for knowledge. Moreover, the cause of education in the Kingdom of Christ is co-ordinate with the causes of missions and general benevolence, and should receive along with these the liberal support of the churches. An adequate system of Christian education is necessary to a complete spiritual program for Christ's people.

"In Christian education there should be a proper balance between academic freedom and academic responsibility. Freedom in any orderly relationship of human life is always limited and never absolute. The freedom of a teacher in a Christian school, college, or seminary is limited by the pre-eminence of Jesus Christ, by the authoritative nature of the Scriptures, and by the distinct purpose for which the school exists."[1]

> **Memory Verses**
>
> "Make Your ways known to me, LORD;
>
> teach me Your paths.
>
> Guide me in Your truth and teach me,
>
> for You are the God of my salvation;
>
> I wait for You all day long." Psalm 25:4-5

"He said to mankind, 'Look! The fear of the Lord—that is wisdom, and to turn from evil is understanding.' "
Job 28:28

"The instruction of the LORD is perfect, reviving the soul; the testimony of the LORD is trustworthy, making the inexperienced wise."
Psalm 19:7

"I have treasured Your word in my heart so that I may not sin against You."
Psalm 119:11

"Christianity is the faith of enlightenment and intelligence." This is an important beginning to a crucial article in *The Baptist Faith and Message*. Some of the people who reject Christianity have suggested that it opposes the life of the mind and education. Nothing could be farther from the truth. As a matter of fact, education stands at the very center of God's assignment to His people.

Enlightenment and Intelligence

Read in the margin the Old Testament Scriptures on education. Then match each reference with the correct summary statement.

____ 1. Job 28:28

____ 2. Psalm 19:7

____ 3. Psalm 119:11

____ 4. Proverbs 3:13

a. Wisdom and understanding bring true happiness.

b. Pure and right, God's law helps you gain wisdom.

c. True wisdom is fearing God, and true understanding is departing from evil.

d. Hiding God's Word in your heart helps protect you from sin.

Did you match the verses 1. c, 2. b, 3. d, 4. a?

128

The psalms instruct us to meditate on and to study the law of God. One of the most central passages about education in the Bible is found in Deuteronomy 4–6, which told the people of Israel that constantly teaching the law of God is a godly responsibility. The particular context for this instruction was parental responsibility within the home. Parents are to teach the law to their children at every opportunity: "when you sit in your house and when you walk along the road, when you lie down and when you get up" (Deut. 6:7). Therefore, the primary responsibility for educating children in the faith lies with parents. Today believers should seize every opportunity as a teachable moment and should constantly teach not only children but all people the Word of God.

> "Happy is a man who finds wisdom and who acquires understanding."
>
> Proverbs 3:13

Mark each statement *T* (true) or *F* (false).

_____ 1. The ancient Jewish home centered on teaching God's Word to children.

_____ 2. The primary responsibility to teach children God's Word today lies with the church.

_____ 3. We should seize every opportunity to teach others God's Word.

_____ 4. God wants His people to study His Word.

Statements 1, 3, and 4 are true; statement 2 is false.

All the Treasures of Wisdom and Knowledge

Christianity is founded on a comprehensive truth claim. At the very heart of the gospel is a call to believe. Thus, a certain knowledge is necessary to be saved, to understand the gospel, and to share the gospel with others. In the earliest centuries of the church, the most important written documents were guides for training new believers and children. These became the church's first theological textbooks.

All truth is God's truth. Christians have nothing to fear from the life of the mind as long as we saturate our minds with God's Word and submit ourselves to His truth as the standard by which all ideologies, philosophies, and truth claims are to be judged (see John 17:17;

"Be diligent to present yourself approved to God, a worker who doesn't need to be ashamed, correctly teaching the word of truth."

2 Timothy 2:15

2 Tim. 2:15). Christianity demands total discipleship, which extends to the life of the mind and to the tasks of learning and teaching.

All truth claims should be judged by (choose one)—
- ☐ the standard of the culture making the truth claim;
- ☐ the individual conscience;
- ☐ God's Word;
- ☐ the local church.

Total discipleship relates (choose one)—
- ☐ exclusively to the mind and to the tasks of learning and teaching;
- ☐ exclusively to the spiritual areas of life;
- ☐ to all of life.

A healthy Christian is characterized by a thirst and desire for knowledge about the gospel and the things of God. To understand the gospel at all is to understand that knowing Christ is the most transforming truth that human beings can know. *The Baptist Faith and Message* succinctly states, "In Jesus Christ abide all the treasures of wisdom and knowledge."

Furthermore, a life of vibrant and healthy discipleship should lead from one stage of knowledge to the next: "He personally gave some to be apostles, some prophets, some evangelists, some pastors and teachers, for the training of the saints in the work of ministry, to build up the body of Christ, until we all reach unity in the faith and in the knowledge of God's Son, growing into a mature man with a stature measured by Christ's fullness. Then we will no longer be little children, tossed by the waves and blown around by every wind of teaching, by human cunning with cleverness in the techniques of deceit. But speaking the truth in love, let us grow in every way into Him who is the head—Christ" (Eph. 4:11-15; also see Heb. 5:12-14).

The New Testament affirms the necessity of spiritual growth with both instruction and warning. Christians are told to seek to know the things of God: "Whatever is true, whatever is honorable, whatever is just, whatever is pure, whatever is lovely, whatever is commendable—

if there is any moral excellence and if there is any praise—dwell on these things" (Phil. 4:8; also see 1 Cor. 2:2). Believers are also warned of the danger of spiritual immaturity. "By this time you ought to be teachers," instructs the Book of Hebrews, warning that Christians who remain in a state of spiritual immaturity and minimal spiritual knowledge are not fulfilling their spiritual discipleship in obedience to Christ (Heb. 5:12).

Read the following New Testament passages on education. Then match each reference with the correct summary statement.

    ___ 1. Matthew 28:19-20   a. A Christian's wisdom is in Christ.

    ___ 2. 1 Corinthians 1:30

    ___ 3. Ephesians 4:11-13   b. We should fill our minds with good things.

    ___ 4. Philippians 4:8

    ___ 5. 2 Timothy 2:15   c. We must win people to faith in Christ and teach them Christian truth.

    d. One of God's gifts to the church is teachers.

    e. We should teach God's Word correctly and give diligence to be approved by God.

You should have matched the passages like this: 1. c, 2. a, 3. d, 4. b, 5. e.

The Liberal Support of the Churches

A local church must take responsibility to organize a comprehensive teaching and training ministry. The central thrust of the church's teaching must come from the pulpit, where Christians are first and foremost to be fed corporately by God's Word in the context of worship through the gift of preaching. In this context the Holy Spirit applies God's Word to believers' hearts, conforming them to the image of the Lord Jesus Christ.

A local church must take responsibility to organize a comprehensive teaching and training ministry.

The church is also charged with organizing and sustaining an educational program that meets the needs of all members. Baptists have long had experience in the programs of Bible study and discipleship. In large part Sunday School began to provide biblical training for young people whose parents were not fulfilling their God-given responsibility. Later, Sunday School expanded into a more comprehensive teaching ministry in the church. Then the discipleship ministry was added to deepen Christians' doctrinal knowledge, to assist their personal spiritual growth, and to equip them for ministry.

Today most churches offer ongoing Bible study in age-graded programs and by other means, and many churches offer topical discipleship studies to develop mature believers. These educational programs help believers of all ages gain a deeper knowledge of the Bible and the Christian life.

Mark each statement T (true) or F (false).

_____ 1. The central thrust of a church's teaching ministry must come through Sunday School.

_____ 2. Sunday School developed in part because parents did not fulfill their God-given responsibility to teach their children.

_____ 3. A discipleship ministry helps believers become more mature believers.

_____ 4. In God's plan, parental teaching is secondary in the church's teaching ministry.

The church's educational responsibility is to undergird the tasks of evangelism, missions, and the other dimensions of Christ's command.

Statements 2 and 3 are true; statements 1 and 4 are false.

The church's educational responsibility is to undergird the tasks of evangelism, missions, and the other dimensions of Christ's command. A church or a denomination cannot sustain a vibrant and faithful missions program if education is not at the heart of its training and preparation of missionaries. For this reason Southern Baptists have established a system of education that includes a wide range of institutions, including many Christian schools, colleges, and universities, along with six theological seminaries. Many Southern Baptist churches sponsor and administer Christian schools. Others encourage and support parents who homeschool their children.

Education undergirds the tasks of evangelism and missions by (check all that apply)—

- ☐ raising the church's awareness of the need for Christian outreach in the immediate and surrounding areas;
- ☐ equipping church members with knowledge and skills to witness effectively;
- ☐ enabling the church to teach members to obey all Jesus commanded;
- ☐ helping the church become aware of the need for Christian missions around the world;
- ☐ preparing new missionaries to carry the gospel to other cultures;
- ☐ helping every believer grow toward Christian maturity.

Education undergirds evangelism and missions in all of these ways.

Academic Freedom and Responsibility

Today's academic culture is characterized by intense debates over academic freedom. In reality, the idea has been corrupted in our times, with many claiming that academic freedom is a license for a teacher or a professor to teach virtually anything he chooses. This idea is far from the Baptist idea of freedom. As *The Baptist Faith and Message* makes clear, "Freedom in any orderly relationship of human life is always limited and never absolute." That is a very important qualification to the idea of academic freedom. The teacher is indeed free but within the boundaries of the institution's mission and confession of faith. This principle has been defined through controversy and at considerable cost. Southern Baptists must expect professors at our institutions to teach in accordance with and not contrary to *The Baptist Faith and Message,* to defend the faith rather than to subvert it, and to inculcate in the next generation a reverent and mature understanding of Christian truth.

Southern Baptists must expect professors at our institutions to defend the faith.

133

The Baptist Faith and Message says, "The freedom of a teacher in a Christian school, college, or seminary is limited by the pre-eminence of Jesus Christ, by the authoritative nature of the Scriptures, and by the distinct purpose for which the school exists." This statement prompted Herschel Hobbs to say, "When a professor accepts a teaching position in any school, he thereby accepts a limitation of personal freedom and the responsibility of teaching within the framework of the general beliefs of the sponsoring body."[2]

Read *The Baptist Faith and Message* article on education, page 127. List three factors that limit the freedom of teachers in Christian schools.

1. _____

2. _____

3. _____

Spend a few minutes thinking about your church's educational ministry. Describe one way that ministry could be strengthened.

_____

_____

_____

Close your study by praying for—
- homes that teach God's truth;
- your church's teaching ministry;
- parents who homeschool their children;
- teachers in Christian and private schools;
- teachers in public schools;
- Baptist colleges and seminaries.

CHAPTER 16

STEWARDSHIP

Article 13
Stewardship

"God is the source of all blessings, temporal and spiritual; all that we have and are we owe to Him. Christians have a spiritual debtorship to the whole world, a holy trusteeship in the gospel, and a binding stewardship in their possessions. They are therefore under obligation to serve Him with their time, talents, and material possessions; and should recognize all these as entrusted to them to use for the glory of God and for helping others. According to the Scriptures, Christians should contribute of their means cheerfully, regularly, systematically, proportionately, and liberally for the advancement of the Redeemer's cause on earth."[1]

> **Memory Verses**
>
> "Don't collect for yourselves treasures on earth, where
>
> moth and rust destroy and where thieves break in and
>
> steal. But collect for yourselves treasures in heaven,
>
> where neither moth nor rust destroys, and where thieves
>
> don't break in and steal. For where your treasure is,
>
> there your heart will be also." Matthew 6:19-21

Stewardship
The responsibility to manage resources God has placed in our care

We cannot understand the biblical vision of the Christian life without embracing the biblical concept of stewardship. This idea goes back to the garden of Eden, where Adam and Eve were assigned the responsibility to be stewards of the garden God had created (see Gen. 1:27-30). At the heart of stewardship is the understanding that stewards do not own what God has entrusted to them but are managers of His resources. As *The Baptist Faith and Message* states, "God is the source of all blessings, temporal and spiritual; all that we have and are we owe to Him." Human beings are granted an incredible responsibility as stewards of God's earth, but this fact is grounded in the principle that God owns everything and that we human beings will give an answer to God for our use, enjoyment, and protection of all He has entrusted to us.

Read each set of Scripture passages on biblical stewardship. Then match each set of references with the correct summary statement.

____ 1. Genesis 1:1; Psalm 24:1; 95:3-5; Haggai 2:8

____ 2. Matthew 25:1-15; 1 Corinthians 4:1

____ 3. Romans 14:12; 1 Corinthians 4:2

a. We are stewards; all we have is held as a trust.

b. We must give account of our stewardship to God.

c. Everything belongs to God.

The correct answers are 1. c, 2. a, 3. b.

The biblical view that God owns all things stands in opposition to modern secularism and the idea of human self-sufficiency. We enjoy a world we did not create. We eat of its fruit, we receive its gifts, and we use its resources—but we have created none of this.

In the New Testament Jesus used the role of a steward in several parables, making clear that we are stewards and as such will give an answer and will be held accountable for our use and investment of what God has given us (see Matt. 25:14-29; Luke 12:16-21; 16:1-13). Being good stewards of what has been entrusted to us is an important Christian responsibility.

A Holy Trusteeship

Christians bear a particular responsibility in stewardship, for as *The Baptist Faith and Message* states, we have received this role as "a holy trusteeship in the gospel." The Bible explains that we have been "bought at a price" (1 Cor. 6:20). Therefore, we belong to Christ, and all that is ours is at Christ's disposal.

The Christian worldview is revolutionary in that it frees people from an unhealthy attachment to material possessions and money. While the world frantically accumulates as much as possible, Christians understand that all earthly goods are to be enjoyed and used only on a temporary basis. Furthermore, we understand that all we are and all we own are at Christ's disposal for the cause of the gospel.

The Apostle Paul explained that Christians are debtors to the entire world (see Rom. 1:14). In other words, those who have received the saving gospel of Christ are commanded to yield and even sacrifice our material possessions for the cause of the gospel so that others may also come to know Christ. Christians must not love the world or the things of the world. Our most valuable possession is the gospel.

In fact, Jesus warned that material possessions can represent an incredible danger for Christians. "You cannot serve God and wealth," Jesus said (Matt. 6:24). Our Lord's point is clear: His redeemed people are to put money, wealth, and material possessions in their proper place and at the disposal of Great Commission priorities.

Read Matthew 6:19-21. Treasures collected on earth (check all that apply)—
□ perish; □ endure; □ bring happiness; □ glorify God.

A Christian can lay up treasures in heaven by (check all that apply)—
□ witnessing to a neighbor;
□ giving to missions;
□ conserving natural resources;
□ feeding a hungry person;
□ saving money;
□ teaching children about God.

"I am obligated both to Greeks and barbarians, both to the wise and the foolish."
Romans 1:14

"Don't collect for yourselves treasures on earth, where moth and rust destroy and where thieves break in and steal. But collect for yourselves treasures in heaven, where neither moth nor rust destroys, and where thieves don't break in and steal. For where your treasure is, there your heart will be also."
Matthew 6:19-21

137

For the Glory of God

Christians are sometimes confused or uncertain about the use of money and material priorities. Some believe that material possessions indicate God's favor. Others trust in material possessions to sustain them in times of need or poverty. A mature Christian understands that material possessions or money cannot buy what is most important—the priceless treasure of salvation through Jesus Christ.

Christian stewardship includes our material possessions but also extends to our energy, our time, and the totality of who we are as human beings. Jesus spoke of a steward's responsibility to exercise talents for the glory of God. The spiritual gifts God bestows on us are not merely for personal edification but are for building up the church. Our stewardship requires us to be ready to give not only our material goods but all that we are for the good of the church and the advancement of the gospel. *The Baptist Faith and Message* reminds us that believers are "under obligation to serve [God] with their time, talents, and material possessions; and should recognize all these as entrusted to them to use for the glory of God and for helping others."

> Christian stewardship extends to our energy, our time, and the totality of who we are.

Each of the following assets comes from God. Identify one way you can be a better steward of each asset. The first one is completed as an example.

My body: *Get a nutritional diet, sufficient exercise, and adequate rest.*

My mind: _____

My abilities: _____

My time: _____

My influence: _____

My spiritual gifts: _____

Christians are to be characterized by generosity. As *The Baptist Faith and Message* states, we are to give "cheerfully, regularly, systematically, proportionately, and liberally" to the cause of Christ. This is a high calling, and those who have not been transformed by the grace of the Lord Jesus Christ would see this requirement as a heavy burden. Yet those who know Jesus Christ as Savior and Lord, who have been adopted as sons and daughters of God, and who know that they are joint heirs with Christ understand that the high calling of Christian stewardship is not a burden but a blessing.

A Christian's stewardship is motivated not by obligation but by a joyful sense of privilege. Those who have received much now have the joy of sharing with others. We give cheerfully, generously, and regularly in obedience to Christ's commands and to other biblical teachings. We honor and worship Christ by giving in His Spirit.

> A Christian's stewardship is motivated not by obligation but by a joyful sense of privilege.

Read each Scripture and match each reference with the correct summary statement.

___ 1. Matthew 6:1-4
___ 2. Matthew 23:23
___ 3. Luke 12:16-21
___ 4. Acts 17:24
___ 5. Acts 20:35
___ 6. 2 Corinthians 9:7
___ 7. Philippians 4:11-12
___ 8. 1 Peter 1:18-19

a. Don't be a show-off in helping others.
b. God made everything and is the Lord of all.
c. God loves a cheerful giver.
d. We should be content with what we have.
e. When tithing, don't neglect justice, mercy, and faith.
f. We were not redeemed with money but with Christ's blood.
g. It is more blessed to give than to receive.
h. It is foolish to store up treasures for yourself and not be rich toward God.

You probably answered this way: 1. a, 2. e, 3. h, 4. b, 5. g, 6. c, 7. d, 8. f.

Ultimately, believers give for the glory of God, but in this life we also give so that the Redeemer's cause on earth will be advanced. This is perhaps the most satisfying motivation for Christian giving.

The Tithe

One issue of controversy among Christians has been the tithe. In the Old Testament God commanded the people of God to give a minimum

> **Tithe**
> One-tenth of a person's income and belongings given to God through the church

139

"Every tenth of the land's produce, grain from the soil or fruit from the trees, belongs to the LORD; it is holy to the LORD. … Every tenth animal from the herd or flock, which passes under the shepherd's rod, will be holy to the LORD."
Leviticus 27:30-32

" 'Bring the full 10 percent into the storehouse,' … says the LORD of Hosts. 'See if I will not open the floodgates of heaven and pour out a blessing for you without measure.' "
Malachi 3:10

of 10 percent as an offering (see Lev. 27:30-32; Mal. 3:10). Some people argue that Christians, no longer under the law, are now free from the responsibility of the tithe. Responsible believers understand, however, that Christians bear no less responsibility for giving than God commanded of His people in the Old Testament. Those who have been transformed by Christ are called to an even higher level of giving that is motivated by more than law and mere obligation (see Matt. 6:19-21; 23:23). Christians must seek to give generously to the local church and to gospel causes, knowing that God loves a cheerful giver (see 2 Cor. 9:7).

Do you agree that Christians should tithe? ☐ Yes ☐ No Why or why not?

_____

Mark each statement _T_ (true) or _F_ (false).
　　___ 1. Not all Christians are stewards.
　　___ 2. A steward does not own what is entrusted to him.
　　___ 3. Material possessions always indicate God's favor.
　　___ 4. We will be held accountable for our use of what God has given us.
　　___ 5. Material possessions can be dangerous for a Christian.
　　___ 6. Christian stewardship is motivated by obligation.

Statements 1, 3, and 6 are false. Statements 2, 4, and 5 are true.

Read _The Baptist Faith and Message_ article on stewardship, page 135. Underline five ways Christians should contribute of their means to advance Christ's work on earth.

Thank God that He has entrusted you as His steward and ask Him to help you be faithful to manage His resources.

CHAPTER 17

COOPERATION

Article 14

Cooperation

"Christ's people should, as occasion requires, organize such associations and conventions as may best secure cooperation for the great objects of the Kingdom of God. Such organizations have no authority over one another or over the churches. They are voluntary and advisory bodies designed to elicit, combine, and direct the energies of our people in the most effective manner. Members of New Testament churches should cooperate with one another in carrying forward the missionary, educational, and benevolent ministries for the extension of Christ's Kingdom. Christian unity in the New Testament sense is spiritual harmony and voluntary cooperation for common ends by various groups of Christ's people. Cooperation is desirable between the various Christian denominations, when the end to be attained is itself justified, and when such cooperation involves no violation of conscience or compromise of loyalty to Christ and His Word as revealed in the New Testament."[1]

> **Memory Verse**
>
> "We are God's co-workers." 1 Corinthians 3:9

The Baptist Faith and Message reminds us that Christian unity is "spiritual harmony and voluntary cooperation for common ends by various groups of Christ's people." Cooperation is not merely an administrative idea conceived in the modern business world. Cooperation doesn't emerge from politics, sociology, or sentimentalism. Instead, our voluntary cooperation as Baptists is grounded in the fact that we share a common salvation and are called to common purposes that can best be accomplished by working together. For Southern Baptists cooperation means a worldwide kingdom work with others who share our faith, values, and worldview.

Cooperation means a worldwide kingdom work with others who share our faith, values, and worldview.

Read the following biblical accounts of cooperation. Match each reference with the kind of cooperation involved. Some kinds of cooperation may be used more than once, while some may not be used at all.

___ 1. Ezra 1:1-4; 2:68-69

___ 2. Nehemiah 4

___ 3. Mark 2:3-4

___ 4. Acts 1:13-14

___ 5. Acts 2:44-47; 4:32-37

___ 6. 1 Corinthians 3:5-11

___ 7. 1 Corinthians 12:4-27

a. Bringing to Jesus a man who needed help

b. Providing for believers in need

c. Preparing to rebuild the temple

d. Prayer

e. Leaders in ministry

f. Serving with spiritual gifts

g. Rebuilding the walls of Jerusalem

The references should be matched this way: 1. c, 2. g, 3. a, 4. d, 5. b, 6. e, 7. f.

The Baptist Faith and Message states that Christians are to "organize such associations and conventions as may best secure cooperation for the great objects of the Kingdom of God." This large, expansive statement is deeply rooted in the Baptist tradition. After all, the very first Baptist churches in London organized themselves into an association. They did this not merely to enjoy fraternal relationships among the churches but to share a mutual accountability to the gospel and to engage in common purposes and a united witness.

Spiritual Harmony and Voluntary Cooperation

Congregationalism is a deeply established Baptist principle. We believe that the primary biblical understanding of the church is a local body of baptized believers that is responsible to God's authority. Yet we understand that just as Christians are not merely individual believers, disconnected from the body of Christ, individual Baptist churches are called to cooperate with other congregations for gospel purposes.

At the same time, the congregational principle reminds us that Baptists are rightly opposed to a hierarchy of any kind. We do not believe that cooperation is established through hierarchical structures that can command the local church or lay claim on its ministry. Thus, Baptists believe in voluntary associations with other like-minded believers. Churches that share a common commitment, convictions, and values voluntarily associate themselves together in order to do in unison what cannot be accomplished alone. Cooperation is always voluntary, never coercive.

Congregationalism
The belief that a local body of believers is directly responsible to God's authority, not to a church hierarchy

Voluntary Association
The united, cooperative effort of churches with common beliefs to minister together in ways they could not minister alone

The concept of congregationalism means (choose one)—
- ☐ the local congregation is directly responsible to the local association;
- ☐ the local congregation is directly responsible to the Southern Baptist Convention;
- ☐ the local congregation is directly responsible to Christ's authority, with no intervening authority.

The concept of voluntary association means (choose one)—
- ☐ churches voluntarily associate together for a common purpose;
- ☐ churches voluntarily associate with missionaries overseas to advance the cause of Christ;
- ☐ churches voluntarily associate with secular organizations for a common purpose.

Because Baptists are congregationalists, we are not responsible to other entities, only to God. However, we voluntarily associate with other Christian groups to achieve a common purpose.

Cooperation for the Great Objects of the Kingdom of God

Our historic Baptist pattern of cooperation reflects the language found in *The Baptist Faith and Message*. Local associations and state conventions, are "voluntary and advisory bodies" rather than authoritative structures. At the same time, these general Baptist bodies are assigned specific responsibilities "to elicit, combine, and direct the energies of our people in the most effective manner"—a statement taken directly from the formation of the Southern Baptist Convention.

This is another important qualification of Baptist cooperation. We cooperate not just for the sake of cooperation but for the sake of accomplishing gospel purposes. Our churches can do together what no one church can do alone. Eliciting, combining, and directing the energies of our people require a mobilization and coordination that start with the local church but are then extended through cooperation with other churches.

> Our churches can do together what no one church can do alone.

Gospel cooperation is a local-church matter. Church members are to cooperate together to fulfill the commission Christ gave His church. As individuals and as congregations, Christians and churches may combine their efforts in missionary, educational, and benevolent ministries. All this is done in the name of Christ for the extension of His kingdom.

Cooperation requires a level of unity beyond a minimal identification with Christ's gospel. True cooperation is grounded in a robust, living faith. Cooperation extends not only from the individual to the church and from churches to general Baptist bodies but also to other Christian denominations. *The Baptist Faith and Message* reminds us that cooperation is desirable between various Christian denominations but only "when the end to be attained is itself justified, and when such cooperation involves no violation of conscience or compromise of loyalty to Christ and His Word as revealed in the New Testament."

This warning explains why Southern Baptists do not join ecumenical organizations and church councils. We believe that true cooperation is grounded in a common commitment to the gospel of the Lord Jesus Christ and in a common obedience to the Bible as the Word of God. Therefore, the Southern Baptist Convention, as a denomination, does not join with churches and other denominations that do not embrace and teach the gospel of Jesus Christ or that do not affirm the Bible as the Word of God.

Check two reasons Southern Baptists have not joined ecumenical organizations and church councils. We do not join with churches that—
☐ do not believe in missions;
☐ do not affirm the Bible as the Word of God;
☐ do not practice baptism by immersion;
☐ do not embrace and teach the gospel of Christ;
☐ do not believe in the premillennial return of Christ.

Why do Baptists join with other Christian groups?

_____

Baptists agree to work with other Christian groups to extend the kingdom of God. We do not cooperate with groups that deny the gospel of Jesus Christ or that do not accept the Bible as the Word of God.

Carrying Forward Missionary, Educational, and Benevolent Ministries

Cooperation, which is woven into our denominational polity and principle, includes our united efforts to undergird and fund Great Commission ministries, such as North American and international missions, and the work of our seminaries and other Southern Baptist programs. Since 1925, Southern Baptists have worked together through the Cooperative Program, the central funding plan for our combined work. The Cooperative Program is recognized as one of the most efficient and effective funding mechanisms in the history

Cooperative Program
A plan of cooperation by which Southern Baptists provide financial support for ministry and missions in an ongoing, systematic way

The Cooperative Program allows local Baptist congregations to unite in a single, unified budget for advancing the cause of Christ.

of organized Christian work, allowing local Baptist congregations to unite in a single, unified budget for advancing the cause of Christ.

M. E. Dodd, who led in developing and adopting the Cooperative Program, said, "The Cooperative Program is intercession in behalf of all our great causes which Christ has committed to our trust. We believe that Southern Baptists should go forward together year by year in high and holy endeavor until His kingdom shall stretch from shore to shore, and His name shall be known from the river to the ends of the earth. ... Money given to the church and the Cooperative Program will go Farther, Rise Higher; Spread Wider, Work Deeper, and Last Longer than when given to any other place or cause."[2]

Louie D. Newton (1892–1986) served as the pastor of Druid Hills Baptist Church in Atlanta, Georgia, for 39 years and served as the president of the Southern Baptist Convention from 1947 to 1948.[3] Newton said in 1947, "The Cooperative Program offers us today, as it has since the hour it was adopted, the surest method of eliciting, combining, and directing the energies of all our people in the propagation of the gospel. It is simple, practical, and scriptural. It has won its way into the confidence of our people. It deserves our complete support in our prayers, our gifts and our loyalty."[4]

Southern Baptists' central funding plan is called the

_____ _____.

Describe two ways your church cooperates with other churches or groups.

1. _____

2. _____

Close your study of this chapter by praying for the work done around the world through the Cooperative Program. Pray that Cooperative Program giving will grow stronger.

CHAPTER 18

THE CHRISTIAN AND THE SOCIAL ORDER

Article 15

The Christian and the Social Order

"All Christians are under obligation to seek to make the will of Christ supreme in our own lives and in human society. Means and methods used for the improvement of society and the establishment of righteousness among men can be truly and permanently helpful only when they are rooted in the regeneration of the individual by the saving grace of God in Jesus Christ. In the spirit of Christ, Christians should oppose racism, every form of greed, selfishness, and vice, and all forms of sexual immorality, including adultery, homosexuality, and pornography. We should work to provide for the orphaned, the needy, the abused, the aged, the helpless, and the sick. We should speak on behalf of the unborn and contend for the sanctity of all human life from conception to natural death. Every Christian should seek to bring industry, government, and society as a whole under the sway of the principles of righteousness, truth, and brotherly love. In order to promote these ends Christians should be ready to work with all men of good will in any good cause, always being careful to act in the spirit of love without compromising their loyalty to Christ and His truth."[1]

Memory Verses

"You are the light of the world. ... Let your light shine before men, so that they may see your good works and give glory to your Father in heaven." Matthew 5:14-16

Christianity authentically relates to the world of society and culture. In other words, Christianity addresses truth to the real world and makes a real difference. As *The Baptist Faith and Message* reminds us, Christians "are under obligation to seek to make the will of Christ supreme in our own lives and in human society." We have a responsibility to our nation, to our society, and to our neighbors. And we understand that the shape and structure of society have much to do with our freedom to proclaim the gospel.

Nevertheless, this responsibility has significant limitations. Christians do not believe that human beings can be transformed by mere social policy or cultural improvement. Only the transforming grace of the Lord Jesus Christ can change a human being and bring about the new birth. As *The Baptist Faith and Message* states, "Means and methods used for the improvement of society and the establishment of righteousness among men can be truly and permanently helpful only when they are rooted in the regeneration of the individual by the saving grace of God in Jesus Christ." At the same time, love of neighbor requires that we genuinely care about the shape of our society—its laws, its customs, and its moral texture.

> Love of neighbor requires that we genuinely care about the shape of our society.

The Establishment of Righteousness

Christians believe that the government has very important responsibilities, including a divine mandate to punish evildoers and to reward those who do right (see Rom. 13:1-7). The good of the commonwealth is necessarily a matter of Christian concern. Thus, when Christians oppose sin, both in individual and in cultural terms, we are motivated by Christian love and concern. Furthermore, we do not speak of sin as if we were not sinners. We speak to the larger society as sinners who have been redeemed and reborn by the power of Christ.

A Christian bears responsibility to engage the political and cultural order and to do so in a way that is distinctively faithful to the commands of Christ. We understand that the church is the eternal people of God and the only institution on earth that will exist in the age to come. Governments and social orders will all pass away, just as history records the rising and falling of countless empires, kingdoms, and nations.

Read Matthew 5:13. Jesus spoke of our responsibility in the world by using the metaphor of _____.

A function of salt is to _____.

Read Matthew 5:14-16. Jesus spoke of our responsibility in the world by using the metaphor of _____.

A function of light is to _____.

What do you think it means for Christians to be salt and light in the world?

_____

_____

"You are the salt of the earth. But if the salt should lose its taste, how can it be made salty? It's no longer good for anything but to be thrown out and trampled on by men."
Matthew 5:13

"You are the light of the world. A city situated on a hill cannot be hidden. No one lights a lamp and puts it under a basket, but rather on a lamp-stand, and it gives light for all who are in the house. In the same way, let your light shine before men, so that they may see your good works and give glory to your Father in heaven."
Matthew 5:14-16

In Jesus' day salt was used to preserve meat. Christians are to have the same purifying influence in society. We are also to reflect Jesus' light in a spiritually dark world.

Christians are to take our social responsibility seriously because it affects the way people live and think. Christian social responsibility holds tremendous power to bless individuals, families, and the larger social order.

The Improvement of Society

The New Testament reveals several specific areas of social responsibility that should be of foremost concern to Christians. *The Baptist Faith and Message* reminds us that we are to oppose racism, greed, selfishness, vice, sexual immorality, and other forms of sin. We do this not only to improve society but also to witness of the grace shown to us in God's law.

Greed. Every generation has been guilty of the sin of greed. In our own day, driven by material ambition and a pervasive consumer culture, greed is an ever-present temptation. Stewardship requires that Christians regard all material goods as belonging to God and that we seek a social order that will achieve a more just society.

People in need. Christians also bear a responsibility to reach out to the less fortunate. The church and individual believers are to minister to the abused, the sick, the poor, and the outcast.

"The Spirit of the Lord is on Me, because He has anointed Me to preach good news to the poor. He has sent Me to proclaim freedom to the captives and recovery of sight to the blind, to set free the oppressed, to proclaim the year of the Lord's favor."
Luke 4:18-19

Jesus has a special place in His heart for people who are rejected by society. Read Luke 4:18-19 and name five ministries Jesus said He was anointed to do.

1. _____
2. _____
3. _____
4. _____
5. _____

Baptist individuals and churches are involved in a wide range of ministries designed to help people with urgent needs. In earlier generations these ministries included hospitals, orphanages, and various institutional programs of human assistance. In more recent years churches, individually and together with other congregations, have developed local assistance programs to individuals and families in need. Through the disaster-relief program of the Southern Baptist Convention's North American Mission Board, millions of people have received help from Southern Baptists at a time of crisis and urgent need.

Read Matthew 25:31-46. Check the truths from this passage.

- ☐ 1. Jesus is concerned about the downtrodden, the poor, and the sick.
- ☐ 2. Jesus expects people to help themselves and not accept help from others.
- ☐ 3. Jesus expects us to help persons in need.
- ☐ 4. Helping someone in need is like helping Jesus.

Numbers 1, 3, and 4 should be checked.

The defenseless. A primary and inescapable Christian responsibility is to speak on behalf of the defenseless. In the New Testament believers were taught to care for the most vulnerable in their culture, widows and orphans (see Jas. 1:27). In our culture Christians must speak on behalf of those who cannot speak for themselves. One important dimension of this task is the church's opposition to abortion.[2] Based on our conviction that all human life is sacred from conception until natural death, Christians must oppose abortion, euthanasia and assisted suicide, human cloning, and any technology or research that involves the destruction of a human embryo. Christians should be at the forefront of efforts to preserve and protect all human life, including the life of the unborn, the aged, the sick, and outcasts of society.

> All human life is sacred from conception until natural death.

Read the following Scriptures about the sanctity of life. Match each reference with the correct summary statement.

- ___ 1. Genesis 1:27
- ___ 2. Exodus 20:13
- ___ 3. Psalm 139:13-16
- ___ 4. Isaiah 44:2,24
- ___ 5. Jeremiah 1:5
- ___ 6. Ephesians 2:10

a. We are made in God's image.

b. Not only did God make us, but He will also help us.

c. God chose His prophet before he was formed in the womb.

d. God created us for good works He planned long ago.

e. Do not kill.

f. God makes us in the womb, and He knows all our days from the beginning.

151

"The gospel of Jesus Christ is a universal remedy from a universal God for the universal need of humanity. The God whom Jesus Christ revealed to the world is not a tribal, national, or racial God. He is for all men of all races, classes, and colors, in all nations and throughout all ages. The gospel is so elemental and fundamental in its application to humanity that it meets the needs of all kinds of persons in all places and at all times."[3]

M. E. Dodd
1878–1952
Pastor, First Baptist Church; Shreveport, Louisiana; president, Southern Baptist Convention, 1934–35

The references should be matched this way: 1. a, 2. e, 3. f, 4. b, 5. c. 6. d.

Racism. The Baptist Faith and Message specifically addresses racism. This sin has been a blight in our nation's history, and Christians bear a particular responsibility to identify racism as a sin that violates the character of God and the unity of humankind as made in God's image. Racism is a grievous sin that Christians are commanded to oppose. Furthermore, racism lies about God's purposes and God's glory. The Book of Revelation paints a vision of the church in which believers are gathered from every tongue and tribe and people and nation (see Rev. 5:9). This prophecy makes clear that God creates and redeems the diverse ethnic cultures found among humanity. Christians must work to ensure that people from every race and language come to a saving knowledge of the Lord Jesus Christ and must welcome people of all races into the body of Christ.

Read the following Scripture passages, which have implications for racism. Match each reference with the correct summary statement.

___ 1. John 3:16

___ 2. Acts 17:26

___ 3. Romans 10:12

___ 4. Revelation 5:9-10

___ 5. Revelation 14:6-7

a. The good news is preached to every tribe and nation.

b. No matter what our background, God is generous to everyone who calls on Him.

c. We all have a common ancestry.

d. People from every language and nation will populate heaven.

e. God loves the entire world; no one is excluded.

You probably answered 1. e, 2. c, 3. b, 4. d. 5. a.

Sexual immorality. Sexual immorality is a matter of widespread controversy in our present day. The sexual revolution has now become institutionalized and is perpetuated through social habits, laws, and customs that are directly at odds with the primacy of marriage and the model of sexual purity that is revealed in the Bible. God takes sex and sexuality with great seriousness. He made humanity in His image as male and female and gave us the gift of sexuality so that His glory could be displayed in the unique covenant of marriage. Sexual immorality, whatever its form, robs God of the glory that is rightfully His through the proper exercise of the sexual gift. Therefore, the Bible expressly prohibits sexual activity outside marriage (see Ex. 20:14; Heb. 13:4).

The misuse, abuse, and corruption of sexuality are tragic hallmarks of modern times. We live in an increasingly pornographic society that celebrates the erotic at the expense of biblical sexuality and marriage. Adultery, homosexuality, cohabitation, premarital sex, and a seemingly endless variety of perversions and sexual sins are celebrated in the larger culture, are featured in entertainment, and are promoted as healthy to the young. Christians must stand without apology against the corruption of God's gift of sexuality and must speak specifically to the Bible's condemnation of sexual sin in every form (see Lev. 18:6,20,22-23; Rom. 1:18-27; 1 Cor. 6:12-20).

> Christians must stand without apology against the corruption of God's gift of sexuality.

Read 1 Corinthians 6:12-20. List two reasons sexual immorality is wrong.

    1. _____

    2. _____

In these verses Paul tells us that our bodies are for the Lord, not for sexual immorality. Because we are one with Christ, we must not commit sexual sin. Our bodies are sanctuaries for the Holy Spirit and belong to God. Therefore, we are to glorify God with our bodies.

One of our greatest challenges today is to speak the truth about the sin of homosexuality. This requires Christian candor, compassion, and courage. We must be as clear as the Bible about the true nature of this sin, even as we reach out to those who are trapped in sinful patterns of behavior with the grace and mercy of Christ. Christians know that sin can be forgiven and lives transformed only through the grace and mercy of our Lord Jesus Christ. Churches should minister to persons struggling with homosexuality and must understand the deep-seated nature of their struggle. The church must simultaneously embody truth and compassion in dealing with this great challenge.

Read Romans 1:18-27. Verses 26-27 teach that homosexuality—
☐ is a sin;   ☐ is natural;   ☐ is approved by God.

The lordship of Jesus Christ extends to every dimension of human work and culture.

The lordship of Jesus Christ extends to every dimension of human work and culture. *The Baptist Faith and Message* instructs that we "should seek to bring industry, government, and society as a whole under the sway of the principles of righteousness, truth, and brotherly love." This incredible task requires our keenest thinking, our most devoted labor, and the mobilization of Christian resources and witness.

To accomplish many of these goals, Christians may join with "all men of good will" in common causes but must always maintain integrity in doctrine and witness. As *The Baptist Faith and Message* reminds us, we must always be careful "to act in the spirit of love without compromising" loyalty to Christ. This is a high standard that requires Christian discernment and mutual accountability.

Name something your church does to help meet the needs of the needy and helpless.

_____

State two actions you can take to become more involved in meeting needs in our society.

1. _____

2. _____

Pray for our society's moral and humanitarian needs. Ask God to guide your involvement in meeting those needs.

CHAPTER 19

PEACE AND WAR

Article 16
Peace and War

"It is the duty of Christians to seek peace with all men on principles of righteousness. In accordance with the spirit and teachings of Christ they should do all in their power to put an end to war.

"The true remedy for the war spirit is the gospel of our Lord. The supreme need of the world is the acceptance of His teachings in all the affairs of men and nations, and the practical application of His law of love. Christian people throughout the world should pray for the reign of the Prince of Peace."[1]

Memory Verse

"If possible, on your part, live at peace with everyone."

Romans 12:18

Conflict and violent confrontation have marked the human experience ever since Adam and Eve were cast out of Eden. Historians estimate that war has been the nearly constant experience of humanity. Periods of widespread peace and freedom from conflict have been all too brief and infrequent. Yet Christians follow the Prince of Peace and are instructed to seek and honor peace.

Seek Peace with All Men

The Baptist Faith and Message states that Christians are "to seek peace with all men on principles of righteousness." Furthermore, "in accordance with the spirit and teachings of Christ they should do all in their power to put an end to war." Even as Christians are to seek peace, we are to do so on principles of righteousness. This significant qualification means that peace is not to be sought at any price—that righteousness must not be sacrificed in the name of false peace.

Righteousness must not be sacrificed in the name of false peace.

The experience of Christians throughout the centuries demonstrates the difficulty of this task and the complexity of understanding how we are to seek peace. Some Christians have adopted pacifism—a total rejection of all armed conflict. To be consistent, pacifists must oppose not only offensive war but any defensive use of force as well. The central problem with pacifism, a minority position in Christian history, is the implication that all uses of force and strength are morally wrong and that Christians must renounce all uses of arms, even to protect others. In effect, a pacifist believes that war or armed conflict of any kind is the worst possible reality.

Most Christians are not strict pacifists. Although they hate war, they see some possibilities as even worse, including the slaughter of innocents, and they see the necessity of war in certain situations.

The position of pacifism (choose one)—
- ☐ rejects all armed conflict;
- ☐ rejects offensive armed conflict only;
- ☐ advocates preemptive war;
- ☐ advocates defensive war only.

At the other extreme, Christians must not love war or glory in armed conflict. Christians cannot wage with earthly weapons the most important war we are called to fight. As Paul reminds us, "Our battle is not against flesh and blood, but against the rulers, against the authorities, against the world powers of this darkness, against the spiritual forces of evil in the heavens" (Eph. 6:12). No Christian wars are fought with earthly weapons and for earthly goals.

> Christians cannot wage with earthly weapons the most important war we are called to fight.

Most Christians have adopted some form of Christian moral realism, a reluctant but honest recognition that armed conflict may sometimes be necessary and may even be morally superior to other options. In general, this understanding takes the form of what theologians and philosophers call the just-war theory. In reality, just-war principles seek to define *war* in such a way that armed conflict would be reduced and peace would more generally prevail—a lasting and righteous peace.

As defined through the centuries, the just-war theory holds that in order for a war or a use of arms to be justified, several criteria must be satisfied. The effort must have a just cause, which means that the use of force must be defensive and never offensive. The force must also be employed with a just intention to secure a fair, lasting peace for all parties. War must also be understood as a last resort, when all other legitimate means of settling a conflict have been tried and have failed. Other principles demand that a just war limit objectives to what is necessary to establish a just peace, that the use of force be approved by legitimate authority, that only proportionate means be used, and that noncombatants be protected whenever possible. There must also be a reasonable chance of success and a realistic hope that the conflict will lead to a superior, lasting peace.

The just-war theory (choose one)—
- ☐ advocates offensive war only;
- ☐ holds that armed conflict should be between equally strong forces;
- ☐ holds that armed conflict may sometimes be necessary and the best option;
- ☐ holds that war is justified only to free the oppressed.

List three criteria for a just war.

1. _____

2. _____

3. _____

Name a war in history that meets the criteria for a just war.

_____

Name a war that does not meet the criteria for a just war.

_____

> "A child will be born for us, a son will be given to us, and the government will be on His shoulders. He will be named Wonderful Counselor, Mighty God, Eternal Father, Prince of Peace."
>
> Isaiah 9:6

> "These will make war against the Lamb, but the Lamb will conquer them because he is Lord of lords and King of kings."
>
> Revelation 17:14

The Reign of the Prince of Peace

Christians understand that war is the result of human sinfulness. Thus, the scourge of war is another reminder of why Christ died and why true and permanent peace can come only when Jesus Christ returns and subjects all powers to His authority. Until then, Christians are to be agents for peace—real, righteous peace.

Jesus is indeed our Prince of Peace (see Isa. 9:6), and the angels at Bethlehem announced Christ's birth by declaring,

> Glory to God in the highest heaven,
> and peace on earth to people He favors!
> Luke 2:14

As *The Baptist Faith and Message* states, "The true remedy for the war spirit is the gospel of our Lord." The ultimate achievement of peace will not come by an international conference or a peace treaty but by the victorious reign of Christ (see Rev. 17:14).

Read Isaiah 2:4 and Micah 4:1-5, which speak of the coming reign of Christ. What will become of disputes among nations under Christ's reign?

_____

What will happen to weapons of war? _____

_____

What will become of training for war? _____

_____

The peace Christ will establish is the peace of His kingdom. Authentic Christian peacemaking takes the form of evangelism and gospel witness, because peace among nations can come only when individuals in those nations come to a saving knowledge of Jesus Christ.

Until Christ comes, we will have war. But Christians must work and contend for peace. We must pray for the reign of the Prince of Peace until He comes.

> We must pray for the reign of the Prince of Peace.

Read the following Scripture passages and match each reference with the correct summary statement.

___ 1. Matthew 5:9

___ 2. Matthew 5:43-48

___ 3. Matthew 26:52

___ 4. Romans 12:18-19

___ 5. James 4:1-2

a. We should seek to live at peace with everyone and not to seek vengeance.

b. We are called to be peacemakers.

c. We are to pray for our enemies and love them.

d. Quarrels and fights come from evil desires within us.

e. Those who fight with the sword will perish by the sword.

You probably answered 1. b, 2. c, 3. e, 4. a, 5. d.

"Blessed are the peacemakers, because they will be called sons of God."
Matthew 5:9

Read Matthew 5:9 again. State a specific way you can be a peacemaker in each of the following areas.

Your home: _____

_____

Your church: _____

_____

Your work: _____

_____

Your community: _____

_____

The world: _____

_____

Ask God to help you be an instrument of His peace.

CHAPTER 20

RELIGIOUS LIBERTY

Article 17
Religious Liberty

"God alone is Lord of the conscience, and He has left it free from the doctrines and commandments of men which are contrary to His Word or not contained in it. Church and state should be separate. The state owes to every church protection and full freedom in the pursuit of its spiritual ends. In providing for such freedom no ecclesiastical group or denomination should be favored by the state more than others. Civil government being ordained of God, it is the duty of Christians to render loyal obedience thereto in all things not contrary to the revealed will of God. The church should not resort to the civil power to carry on its work. The gospel of Christ contemplates spiritual means alone for the pursuit of its ends. The state has no right to impose penalties for religious opinions of any kind. The state has no right to impose taxes for the support of any form of religion. A free church in a free state is the Christian ideal, and this implies the right of free and unhindered access to God on the part of all men, and the right to form and propagate opinions in the sphere of religion without interference by the civil power."[1]

> **Memory Verses**
>
> "I urge that petitions, prayers, intercessions, and thanksgivings be made for everyone, for kings and all those who are in authority, so that we may lead a tranquil and quiet life in all godliness and dignity." 1 Timothy 2:1-2

Religious liberty has always been a Baptist principle and a Baptist passion. As Herschel Hobbs explained, "Religious liberty is the mother of all true freedom."[2] Our commitment is to religious liberty for all peoples, not just for Baptists, because we believe that every human being is created in God's image and possesses full rights and freedoms granted by the Creator, as well as full accountability.

Lord of the Conscience

Religious liberty is not a gift of the U.S. Constitution but the gift of God. The very fact that God created humans as moral and spiritual beings, possessing a moral conscience, indicates that God intends for His human creatures to be both free and responsible.

"You will know the truth, and the truth will set you free."
John 8:32

"If the Son sets you free, you really will be free."
John 8:36

"Peter and John answered them, 'Whether it's right in the sight of God for us to listen to you rather than to God, you decide; for we are unable to stop speaking about what we have seen and heard.' "
Acts 4:19-20

Read the following Scripture passages in the margin.
Match each reference with the correct summary statement.

___ 1. John 8:32   a. God should have first place in our allegiance.
___ 2. John 8:36   b. True freedom comes from Jesus Christ.
___ 3. Acts 4:19-20   c. People are set free by God's truth.
___ 4. Philippians 3:20   d. The Christian's primary citizenship is in heaven.

"Our citizenship is in heaven, from which we also eagerly wait for a Savior, the Lord Jesus Christ."
Philippians 3:20

Did you respond this way: 1. c, 2. b, 3. a, 4. d?

Early Baptists suffered intense persecution and hostility, which taught Baptists to recognize the necessity of authentic religious liberty. Roger Williams (c. 1603–83) was not the only early Baptist to feel the sting of persecution. Obadiah Holmes (c. 1607–82) left England and came to Massachusetts for religious freedom. After a dozen years Holmes found the persecution in the new land unbearable and moved to the wilderness area of Newport, Rhode Island. He became the assistant to John Clarke, the pastor of the Baptist church in Newport.[3]

In July 1651 John Clarke, Obadiah Holmes, and another man traveled 80 miles to Lynn, Massachusetts, to see a blind, aged fellow Baptist.

While conducting a worship service in the man's home, the three men were rudely arrested and sent to Boston for trial. They were ordered either to pay a considerable fine or to be publicly whipped. Sympathizers raised money to pay the fines of Clarke and the third man, but Holmes, as a matter of principle, refused to let anyone pay his fine.

Holmes was held in jail until September 5 and then taken to the public whipping post. Stripped to the waist and tied to the post, Holmes received 30 heavy strokes with a three-cord whip, wielded by the executioner with both hands. Holmes's back turned to a bloody mass of torn flesh. He was beaten so badly that he had to sleep on his hands and knees for weeks afterward, unable to lie down.[4]

Religious liberty is not mere legal toleration. Instead, it is the recognition that the very nature of humanity implies respect for this right and liberty. No government has the right to claim coercive power over any individual's conscience in matters of faith and religious belief.

George Truett preached a message from the steps of the United States capital in 1920 to a crowd estimated by J. B. Gambrell to be between 10,000 and 15,000 people.[5] In his timeless message Truett said, "It is the natural and fundamental and indefeasible right of every human being to worship God or not, according to the dictates of his conscience, and, as long as he does not infringe upon the rights of others, he is to be held accountable alone to God for all religious beliefs and practices. Our contention is not for mere toleration, but for absolute liberty. There is a wide difference between toleration and liberty. ... Toleration is a matter of expediency, while liberty is a matter of principle. Toleration is a gift from man, while liberty is a gift from God. ... God wants free worshipers and no other kind."[6]

The Baptist Faith and Message begins with the affirmation that "God alone is Lord of the conscience, and He has left it free from the doctrines and commandments of men which are contrary to His Word or not contained in it." This statement introduces a very important fact: we are not free from the commandments and doctrines of God's Word but from the dictates and commandments of earthly powers that are in any way contrary to God's Word.

In other words, human beings are not really autonomous. We will one day answer to God for our beliefs, actions, thoughts, and words.

> No government has the right to claim coercive power over any individual's conscience in matters of faith and religious belief.

Our modern culture, especially in the developed nations, increasingly sees humanity as fully autonomous, with every individual totally free to define his or her own existence. This is not a biblical understanding of human freedom. Although the Bible charges Christians to respect governing authorities (see Rom. 13:1-7), government has no right to demand ultimate allegiance. But God does (see Matt. 22:21).

"Give back to Caesar the things that are Caesar's, and to God the things that are God's."
Matthew 22:21

A Free Church in a Free State

The Baptist Faith and Message also asserts that church and state should be separate. This is an institutional principle that protects both church and state. Baptists resist the idea of a state church and have resisted and rejected the idea that the church should rely on the state to accomplish its gospel mandate and ministry. J. B. Gambrell wrote, "We … hold with unshaken confidence to the age-long contention of Baptists that there must be absolute separation between church and state, and that the right of civil and religious liberty is, in the sight of God, the inalienable and indefeasible right of every human being."[7] Louie D. Newton wrote, "Baptists have, in every age, stood stoutly and fearlessly and, at times, sacrificially, for religious liberty and its inevitable corollary, the complete separation of church and state."[8]

"*Every man must give an account of himself to God, and therefore every man ought to be at liberty to serve God in a way that he can best reconcile to his conscience. If government can answer for individuals at the day of judgment, let men be controlled by it in religious matters; otherwise, let men be free.*"[9]
John Leland
1754–1841
Baptist minister

At the same time, the modern idea generally described in the larger culture as the separation of church and state most often means an artificial exclusion of all religious belief and expression from the public square. Some courts and other authorities have imposed an open hostility toward religion, often driven by advocates of a radical form of secularism. Baptists must insist that the church should be independent of the state, but we must also insist that the state must not be hostile to the church or to the free and full participation of all citizens—including Christians—in the public life of the nation. Baptists must counter any hostility toward religious expression on the basis of historic Baptist principles. Christians must be free to bring their biblically informed understanding of moral truth to the nation's public policy debates as the salt and the light that Christ has commanded them to be (see Matt. 5:13-16), even as they contend for full religious liberty for all citizens, whatever their faith.

The Baptist Faith and Message expresses the Baptist understanding that the state owes every church "protection and full freedom in the pursuit of its spiritual ends." In other words, the rights of all religious groups must be respected and protected—even the rights of religious minorities and unpopular religious movements. No church is to be preferred over another. Because Baptists suffered persecution under governments that had established state-privileged churches, we have been ardent proponents of true, nonpreferential religious liberty.

John Smyth wrote, "The magistrate is not by virtue of his office to meddle with religion, or matters of conscience."[10] One record indicates that Smyth spent time in an English prison because of his refusal to conform his views to the teachings of the Church of England.[11] Thomas Helwys (c. 1550–c. 1616) worked with John Smyth to form the first Baptist church in modern history. In 1612 Helwys returned to England and began the first Baptist church on English soil. Helwys, an ardent supporter of religious freedom, also suffered imprisonment for his stand. He wrote, "Mens religion to God, is betwixt God and themselves; the King shall not answer for it, neither may the King be judg betwene God and man."[13]

The Baptist Faith and Message rightly stipulates that "the gospel of Christ contemplates spiritual means alone for the pursuit of its ends." This is a very important principle. The church must be free to fulfill its gospel ministry as assigned by Christ, and it must fulfill that ministry without interference or assistance from the state.

> *"Religion is a matter between God and man. The state has no authority in the religious sphere. Equal freedom for all religious beliefs and equal protection to all is the Baptist ideal. Legislation favoring one denomination or one religion more than others is foreign to the Baptist conception."[12]*
>
> E. Y. Mullins
> 1860–1928
> President, the Southern Baptist Theological Seminary

Read *The Baptist Faith and Message* article on religious liberty, page 161. List two things the state owes every church.

1. _____

2. _____

Loyal Obedience

Religious liberty also requires that Christian citizens obey the government and its laws. Jesus instructed His disciples to "give back to Caesar the things that are Caesar's, and to God the things that are God's" (Matt. 22:21). This means that Christians, like other citizens, must pay taxes and obey the laws of the state.

Governing authorities serve God by requiring obedience to law and respect for authority.

Paul expanded on this point, instructing believers that Christians are to "submit to the governing authorities" (Rom. 13:1). He explained that governing authorities serve God by requiring obedience to law and respect for authority; "therefore, you must submit, not only because of wrath, but also because of your conscience" (Rom. 13:5). The government has a right to tax, as well as a right and responsibility to maintain order and to protect its citizens. But no government has the right to coerce the conscience or to persecute citizens because of their religious convictions.

Read the following Scripture passages and match each passage with the correct summary statement.

    ___ 1. Romans 13:1-7

    ___ 2. 1 Timothy 2:1-2

    ___ 3. 1 Peter 2:13-17

a. We should honor civil authorities.

b. We should pray for civil authorities.

c. We should submit to civil authorities and pay taxes.

The references should be matched this way: 1. c, 2. b, 3. a.

E. Y. Mullins once defined the Baptist concept as "a free church in a free state."[14] These words remind Baptists of our responsibility to protect, defend, and contend for religious liberty at home and around the world. This is part of our Baptist witness and our gospel task.

Review this chapter and list three Baptist leaders who worked for religious liberty.

    1. _____

    2. _____

    3. _____

Thank God for your religious freedom and for the early Baptists who paid dearly for it. Pray for the peoples of the world who do not have religious freedom.

CHAPTER 21

THE FAMILY

Article 18

The Family

"God has ordained the family as the foundational institution of human society. It is composed of persons related to one another by marriage, blood, or adoption.

"Marriage is the uniting of one man and one woman in covenant commitment for a lifetime. It is God's unique gift to reveal the union between Christ and His church and to provide for the man and the woman in marriage the framework for intimate companionship, the channel of sexual expression according to biblical standards, and the means for procreation of the human race.

"The husband and wife are of equal worth before God, since both are created in God's image. The marriage relationship models the way God relates to His people. A husband is to love his wife as Christ loved the church. He has the God-given responsibility to provide for, to protect, and to lead his family. A wife is to submit herself graciously to the servant leadership of her husband even as the church willingly submits to the headship of Christ. She, being in the image of God as is her husband and thus equal to him, has the God-given responsibility to respect her husband and to serve as his helper in managing the household and nurturing the next generation.

"Children, from the moment of conception, are a blessing and heritage from the Lord. Parents are to demonstrate to their children God's pattern for marriage. Parents are to teach their children spiritual and moral values and to lead them, through consistent lifestyle example and loving discipline, to make choices based on biblical truth. Children are to honor and obey their parents."[1]

Memory Verse

"Be kind and compassionate to one another, forgiving one another, just as God also forgave you in Christ."

Ephesians 4:32

Family
Persons related by marriage, blood, or adoption

"The man said: This one, at last, is bone of my bone, and flesh of my flesh; this one will be called woman, for she was taken from man. This is why a man leaves his father and mother and bonds with his wife, and they become one flesh."
Genesis 2:23-24

Confusion over the nature of the family has produced a context of great danger in modern times. Few confessions of faith throughout the history of the church included articles on marriage and the family because Christians through the centuries have been united in a common understanding of God's plan for marriage, family, and children. In adding this article to *The Baptist Faith and Message* in 1998, Southern Baptists boldly declared a commitment to the biblical vision of the family as our standard and witness.

The Foundational Institution

The modern secular concept of the family is largely driven by sociological theories and assumes that marriage and the traditional family structure are merely the products of human social evolution. Thus, proponents of the secular view believe that because the family is simply a sociological development, it can be renegotiated and restructured to meet modern expectations.

Christians must insist otherwise. We believe marriage, which was instituted by God before the fall, was a central part of God's design for humanity from the beginning (see Gen. 2:23-24). Furthermore, we believe the family, consisting of a mother, a father, and their children, reflects God's glory in the right ordering of civilization and society.

Refer to the first paragraph of *The Baptist Faith and Message* article on the family, page 167. Underline the definition of *family*.

168

The Baptist Faith and Message affirms that God ordained the family "as the foundational institution of human society." This truth directly refutes modern society's assumption that the basic unit of civilization is the autonomous individual. Helpfully, *The Baptist Faith and Message* also defines *family* as "composed of persons related to one another by marriage, blood, or adoption." This correctly identifies the family as a central part of God's design for humanity.

The biblical definition of *family* is expanded through ties of marriage, blood, and adoption through many generations and through various relatives who compose an extended family. All people—married or unmarried—are thus related to family through various ties of blood, kinship, and adoption. We are husbands and wives, mothers and fathers, sons and daughters, brothers and sisters, as well as part of a larger extended family.

In our confused times many people celebrate what is described as a diversity of family forms. Although Christians recognize that families can experience brokenness, we must also assert that God's purpose and intention are that we build, nurture, and respect ties of marriage, blood, and adoption. The family is not a laboratory for social experimentation but an arena in which God's glory is shown to the world in the right ordering of human relationships.

One Man and One Woman

What is marriage? "Marriage is the uniting of one man and one woman in covenant commitment for a lifetime." That simple declarative statement from *The Baptist Faith and Message* stands on a firm biblical foundation and expresses God's design for marriage as a covenant that unites one man and one woman in a lifelong union marked by fidelity and mutuality (see Heb. 13:4).

God honored marriage by establishing the metaphor of the bridegroom and the bride to express the relationship between Christ and His church. Christ's redeemed people are described as the bride, and the Lord Jesus Christ is the Bridegroom (see Rev. 19:7). This metaphor helps us understand the intimacy, purity, and order that are to characterize earthly marriages.

> **Marriage**
> The uniting of one man and one woman in covenant commitment for a lifetime

> "Marriage must be respected by all, and the marriage bed kept undefiled, because God will judge immoral people and adulterers."
> Hebrews 13:4

> "Let us be glad, rejoice, and give Him glory, because the marriage of the Lamb has come, and His wife has prepared herself."
> Revelation 19:7

Refer to the second paragraph in the article on the family, page 167. Underline the definition of *marriage*. List the four purposes of marriage.

1. _____

2. _____

3. _____

4. _____

> "Husbands, love your wives, just as also Christ loved the church and gave Himself for her."
>
> Ephesians 5:25

> "Wives, be submissive to your husbands, as is fitting in the Lord. Husbands, love your wives and don't become bitter against them. Children, obey your parents in everything, for this is pleasing in the Lord. Fathers, do not exasperate your children, so they won't become discouraged."
>
> Colossians 3:18-21

Human sexuality is one of the most explosive forces on earth. The Bible establishes marriage as the only proper arena for and channel of sexual expression. Thus, God's wonderful gift of sex is invested in marriage and the one-flesh relationship that is established between husband and wife. The shared gift of intimacy, which is a blessing to a husband and a wife within the marital covenant, can only lead to destruction and heartbreak outside marriage (see 1 Cor. 7:1-16).

The gift of sex is intended to strengthen the marital bond and to affirm the exclusiveness of the relationship between the husband and the wife. The Bible affirms that the gift of sex is meant for pleasure only within the confines and context of marriage. Only in the one-flesh relationship can sex find its proper place and be received as the gift God intended it to be. The Bible also teaches and *The Baptist Faith and Message* affirms that sex is "the means for procreation of the human race" (see Gen. 1:28).

Number in the previous paragraph the four reasons God gave the gift of sex.

The Baptist Faith and Message wonderfully affirms that both "husband and wife are of equal worth before God" and explains that both the man and the woman are created in God's image (see Gen. 1:27). Referring to the bride-and-bridegroom metaphor, *The Baptist Faith and Message* also reminds husbands of their responsibility to love their wives as Christ loved the church (see Eph. 5:25). Husbands are assigned the responsibility to provide for their families and to protect them from harm. Husbands are also assigned to be leaders in the marriage and the family (see Col. 3:18-21).

170

Article 3 in *The Baptist Faith and Message* reminded us that "the gift of gender is ... part of the goodness of God's creation." This truth flies directly in the face of modern theories of gender. The presupposition of our postmodern culture is that gender is simply a social construction and that differences between men and women result from oppression or historical maladjustment. The Bible insists otherwise. As *The Baptist Faith and Message* explains, "A wife is to submit herself graciously to the servant leadership of her husband even as the church willingly submits to the headship of Christ" (see Eph. 5:22-33). The biblical concept of submission does not mean that the wife has no influence in family decision making or that her contribution is depreciated or denied. On the contrary, the biblical idea of submission points to the wife's role in glorifying God by honoring the role God has assigned the husband. The husband is to devote himself to his wife and family and exercise his responsibility to lead, not on the basis of dictatorial power but on the basis of spiritual authority as demonstrated in his faithfulness to Christ. The husband is obligated to give himself in sacrificial service to his wife and family.

The Baptist Faith and Message stipulates that the wife, "being in the image of God as is her husband," is "thus equal to him," even as she receives "the God-given responsibility to respect her husband and to serve as his helper in managing the household and nurturing the next generation." As the Bible makes abundantly clear, motherhood is to be greatly honored and respected, and the proper relationship between the husband and the wife produces family harmony and provides a witness to the glory of God. After all, the New Testament points to marriage as the picture of the relationship between Christ and His bride, the church (see Eph. 5:23-27). A healthy Christian marriage is a powerful illustration of the gospel.

> The proper relationship between the husband and the wife produces family harmony and provides a witness to the glory of God.

A Blessing and Heritage

The Bible reveals that children are to be received as blessings and gifts from God. Children are not to be seen as an imposition on the marriage but as blessings that promise a heritage from the Lord (see Prov. 17:6). *The Baptist Faith and Message* states that parents are "to teach their children spiritual and moral values." Parents are to raise their children "in the training and instruction of the Lord" (Eph. 6:4). This is a demanding task in our confusing times, but parents are to lead children "through consistent lifestyle example and loving discipline" so that they will make choices and decisions "based on biblical truth" (see Prov. 22:6,15; 23:13-15; 29:17; Eph. 6:1-4).

> [1]"Children, obey your parents in the Lord, because this is right. [2]'Honor your father and mother'— which is the first commandment with a promise— [3] 'that it may go well with you and that you may have a long life in the land.' [4]And fathers, don't stir up anger in your children, but bring them up in the training and instruction of the Lord."
>
> Ephesians 6:1-4

Read Ephesians 6:1-4 in the margin. Match each reference with the correct summary statement.

___ Verse 1   a. Children owe their parents honor.

___ Verse 2   b. Children owe their parents obedience.

___ Verse 4   c. Parents should raise their children in the instruction of the Lord.

The primary responsibilities of nurturing the family and raising children are assigned to the husband and wife. Children are also assigned responsibility to honor and obey their parents, for this is pleasing to God and is a testimony to God's loving purpose for the family.

We live in a time when the definition of *family* is a matter of political and social controversy and when the culture is confused about the definition of *marriage*. Christians bear the unique responsibility to tell the truth, to live the truth, and to bear witness to God's loving intention in establishing marriage and the family for our good. God gave us marriage and family for our happiness and our health, but He also created them as structures of accountability so that we can live holy lives, demonstrating His character, love, and wisdom as we fulfill all the responsibilities and roles assigned to marriage and the family.

What are two specific actions you can take to strengthen your marriage and your family?

1. _____

2. _____

Pray that God will strengthen homes and will help Christian families be all He wants them to be.

NOTES

Chapter 1

1. *The Baptist Faith and Message: A Statement Adopted by the Southern Baptist Convention, June 14, 2000* (Nashville: LifeWay Press, 2000), 7. See Exodus 24:4; Deuteronomy 4:1-2; 17:19; Joshua 8:34; Psalms 19:7-10; 119:11,89,105,140; Isaiah 34:16; 40:8; Jeremiah 15:16; 36:1-32; Matthew 5:17-18; 22:29; Luke 21:33; 24:44-46; John 5:39; 16:13-15; 17:17; Acts 2:16ff.; 17:11; Romans 15:4; 16:25-26; 2 Timothy 3:15-17; Hebrews 1:1-2; 4:12; 1 Peter 1:25; 2 Peter 1:19-21.

2. C. H. Spurgeon, *The New Park Street Pulpit*, vol. 1 (Pasadena, TX: Pilgrim Publications, 1981), 110.

3. Joseph Powhatan Cox, "Manly, Basil Jr.," in *Encyclopedia of Southern Baptists*, vol. 2 (Nashville: Broadman Press, 1958), 817–18.

4. Timothy and Denise George, eds., *Basil Manly Jr.: The Bible Doctrine of Inspiration* (Nashville: Broadman and Holman Publishers, 1995), 53.

5. M. E. Dodd, *The Democracy of the Saints* (Nashville: Sunday School Board of the Southern Baptist Convention, 1924), 75.

6. J. L. Dagg, *Manual of Theology* (Harrisonburg, VA: Gano Books, 1990), 23.

7. James T. Draper Jr., *We Believe: Living in the Light of God's Truth* (Nashville: LifeWay Press, 2003), 9.

8. W. A. Criswell, *Standing on the Promises: The Autobiography of W. A. Criswell* (Dallas: Word, 1990), 132.

9. Ibid., 234.

10. Herschel H. Hobbs, *My Faith and Message: An Autobiography* (Nashville: Broadman & Holman Publishers, 1993), 81.

11. Billy Graham, *Just as I Am: The Autobiography of Billy Graham* (New York: HarperCollins Publishers, 1997), 139.

12. Ibid.

13. Billy Graham, letter to the editor, *Newsweek*, 4 September 2006, 22.

14. Adrian Rogers, *What Every Christian Should Know* (Nashville: Broadman & Holman Publishers, 2005), 234.

15. Timothy and Denise George, eds., *J. M. Frost: Baptist Why and Why Not* (Nashville: Broadman & Holman Publishers, 1996), 17–18.

16. B. H. Carroll, *Inspiration of the Bible* (Nashville: Thomas Nelson Publishers, 1980), 121.

17. Kenneth Boa, *Historic Creeds: A Journal* (Colorado Springs: NavPress, 2000), 12–23.

Chapter 2

1. *The Baptist Faith and Message* statement, 7.

2. E. Y. Mullins, *Baptist Beliefs* (Valley Forge, PA: Judson Press, 1925), 17.

3. Thomas O. Chisholm, "Great Is Thy Faithfulness," in *The Baptist Hymnal* (Nashville: Convention Press, 1991), 54.

4. Walter Martin, *The Kingdom of the Cults* (Minneapolis: Bethany House Publishers, 2003), 72–73, 168–70, 238.

5. James Leo Garrett Jr., *Systematic Theology: Biblical, Historical, and Evangelical* (North Richland Hills, TX: BIBAL Press, 2000), 331–33.

6. Dagg, *Manual of Theology*, 250.

7. Ibid., 249.

8. Mullins, *Baptists Beliefs*, 19–20.

9. Draper, *We Believe*, 15.

10. Herschel H. Hobbs, *What Baptists Believe* (Nashville: Broadman Press, 1964), 14.

Chapter 3

1. *The Baptist Faith and Message* statement, 8. See Genesis 1:1; 2:7; Exodus 3:14; 6:2-3; 15:11ff.; 20:1ff.; Leviticus 22:2; Deuteronomy 6:4; 32:6; 1 Chronicles 29:10; Psalm 19:1-3; Isaiah 43:3,15; 64:8; Jeremiah 10:10; 17:13; Matthew 6:9ff.; 7:11; 23:9; 28:19; Mark 1:9-11; John 4:24; 5:26; 14:6-13; 17:1-8; Acts 1:7; Romans 8:14-15; 1 Corinthians 8:6; Galatians 4:6; Ephesians 4:6; Colossians 1:15; 1 Timothy 1:17; Hebrews 11:6; 12:9; 1 Peter 1:17; 1 John 5:7.

2. Timothy George and David S. Dockery, *Theologians of the Baptist Tradition* (Nashville: Broadman and Holman, 2001), 91–97; John A. Broadus, *Commentary on Matthew* (Grand Rapids: Kregel Classics, 1990), 135.

3. Hobbs, *What Baptists Believe*, 24.

4. Ibid., 26.

Chapter 4

1. *The Baptist Faith and Message* statement, 8–9. See Genesis 18:1ff.; Psalms 2:7ff.; 110:1ff.; Isaiah 7:14; 53; Matthew 1:18-23; 3:17; 8:29; 11:27; 14:33; 16:16,27; 17:5; 27; 28:1-6,19; Mark 1:1; 3:11; Luke 1:35; 4:41; 22:70; 24:46; John 1:1-18,29; 10:30,38; 11:25-27; 12:44-50; 14:7-11; 16:15-16,28; 17:1-5,21-22; 20:1-20,28; Acts 1:9; 2:22-24; 7:55-56; 9:4-5,20; Romans 1:3-4; 3:23-26; 5:6-21; 8:1-3,34; 10:4; 1 Corinthians 1:30; 2:2; 8:6; 15:1-8,24-28; 2 Corinthians 5:19-21; 8:9; Galatians 4:4-5; Ephesians 1:20; 3:11; 4:7-10; Philippians 2:5-11; Colossians 1:13-22; 2:9; 1 Thessalonians 4:14-18; 1 Timothy 2:5-6; 3:16;

Titus 2:13-14; Hebrews 1:1-3; 4:14-15; 7:14-28; 9:12-15,24-28; 12:2; 13:8; 1 Peter 2:21-25; 3:22; 1 John 1:7-9; 3:2; 4:14-15; 5:9; 2 John 7-9; Revelation 1:13-16; 5:9-14; 12:10-11; 13:8; 19:16.

2. Vernon Latrelle Stanfield, ed., *Favorite Sermons of John A. Broadus* (New York: Harper & Brothers Publishers, 1959), 53.

3. Dagg, *Manual of Theology*, 179.

4. Draper, *We Believe,* 16.

5. Robert G. Lee, *The Sinner's Saviour* (Nashville: Broadman Press, 1950), 31.

6. Robert G. Lee, *Beds of Pearls* (Grand Rapids, MI: Zondervan Publishing House, 1936), 36–37.

7. W. A. Criswell, ed., *The Criswell Study Bible* (Nashville: Thomas Nelson, Publishers, 1979), 1327.

8. Stanfield, *Favorite Sermons,* 91.

9. Timothy and Denise George, eds., *John A. Broadus: Baptist Confessions, Covenants, and Catechisms* (Nashville: Broadman & Holman Publishers, 1996), 269.

10. Robert G. Lee, *Salvation in Christ* (Grand Rapids: Zondervan Publishing House, 1961), 14.

11. Dagg, *Manual of Theology,* 233.

12. Stanfield, *Favorite Sermons,* 88.

13. Truett, *Who Is Jesus?* (Grand Rapids, MI: Baker Book House, 1952), 164.

14. Broadus, *Commentary on Matthew* (Grand Rapids: Kregel Classics, 1990), 589.

15. Jerry Vines, *Great Events in the Life of Christ* (Wheaton, IL: Victor Books, 1979), 117–18.

16. M. E. Dodd, *The Christ Whom We Worship* (Shreveport, LA: The Journal Publishing Co., 1930), 106.

17. R. Albert Mohler, comp., Timothy and Denise George, eds., *E. Y. Mullins: The Axioms of Religion* (Nashville: Broadman & Holman Publishers, 1997), 185.

Chapter 5

1. *The Baptist Faith and Message* statement, 9. See Genesis 1:2; Judges 14:6; Job 26:13; Psalms 51:11; 139:7ff.; Isaiah 61:1-3; Joel 2:28-32; Matthew 1:18; 3:16; 4:1; 12:28-32; 28:19; Mark 1:10,12; Luke 1:35; 4:1,18-19; 11:13; 12:12; 24:49; John 4:24; 14:16-17,26; 15:26; 16:7-14; Acts 1:8; 2:1-4,38; 4:31; 5:3; 6:3; 7:55; 8:17,39; 10:44; 13:2; 15:28; 16:6; 19:1-6; Romans 8:9-11, 14-16,26-27; 1 Corinthians 2:10-14; 3:16; 12:3-11,13; Galatians 4:6; Ephesians 1:13-14; 4:30; 5:18; 1 Thessalonians 5:19; 1 Timothy 3:16; 4:1; 2 Timothy 1:14; 3:16; Hebrews 9:8,14; 2 Peter 1:21; 1 John 4:13; 5:6-7; Revelation 1:10; 22:17.

2. W. A. Criswell, *Great Doctrines of the Bible*, vol. 4, *Pneumatology* (Grand Rapids: Zondervan Publishing House, 1984), 16.

3. W. A Criswell, *The Holy Spirit in Today's World* (Grand Rapids: Zondervan Publishing House, 1966), 54, 57.

4. Edwin Hatch, "Breathe on Me," in *The Baptist Hymnal,* 238.

Chapter 6

1. *The Baptist Faith and Message* statement, 8–9. Genesis 1:26-30; 2:5,7,18-22; 3; 9:6; Psalms 1; 8:3-6; 32:1-5; 51:5; Isaiah 6:5; Jeremiah 17:5; Matthew 16:26; Acts 17:26-31; Romans 1:19-32; 3:10-18,23; 5:6,12,19; 6:6; 7:14-25; 8:14-18,29; 1 Corinthians 1:21-31; 15:19, 21-22; Ephesians 2:1-22; Colossians 1:21-22; 3:9-11.

2. W. T. Conner, *Christian Doctrine* (Nashville: Broadman Press, 1937), 22.

3. Mullins, *Baptist Beliefs,* 24.

Chapter 7

1. *The Baptist Faith and Message* statement, 19. See Genesis 3:15; Exodus 3:14-17; 6:2-8; Matthew 1:21; 4:17; 16:21-26; 27:22–28:6; Luke 1:68-69; 2:28-32; John 1:11-14,29; 3:3-21,36; 5:24; 10:9,28-29; 15:1-16; 17:17; Acts 2:21; 4:12; 15:11; 16:30-31; 17:30-31; 20:32; Romans 1:16-18; 2:4; 3:23-25; 4:3ff.; 5:8-10; 6:1-23; 8:1-18,29-39; 10:9-10,13; 13:11-14; 1 Corinthians 1:18,30; 6:19-20; 15:10; 2 Corinthians 5:17-20; Galatians 2:20; 3:13; 5:22-25; 6:15; Ephesians 1:7; 2:8-22; 4:11-16; Philippians 2:12-13; Colossians 1:9-22; 3:1ff.; 1 Thessalonians 5:23-24; 2 Timothy 1:12; Titus 2:11-14; Hebrews 2:1-3; 5:8-9; 9:24-28; 11:1–12:8,14; James 2:14-26; 1 Peter 1:2-23; 1 John 1:6–2:11; Revelation 3:20; 21:1–22:5.

2. W. A. Criswell, *Great Doctrines of the Bible*, vol. 5, *Soteriology* (Grand Rapids: Zondervan Publishing House, 1985), 54.

3. Conner, *Christian Doctrine*, 162.

4. Timothy George, *Amazing Grace* (Nashville: LifeWay Press, 2000), 21.

5. Ibid., 10.

6. Ibid., 13, 24.

7. Herschel H. Hobbs, *The Baptist Faith and Message, Revised Edition* (Nashville: Convention Press, 1971), 52.

8. Rogers, *What Every Christian Should Know*, 35.

9. Timothy and Denise George, eds., *B. H. Carroll: Baptists and Their Doctrines* (Nashville: Broadman and Holman Publishers, 1999), 119.

10. George, *John A. Broadus*, 271.

11. L. R. Scarborough, *Prepare to Meet God* (Nashville: Sunday School Board of the Southern Baptist Convention, 1922), 10–11.

12. Jewell Mae Daniel, *The Chimes of Shreveport: The Life of M. E. Dodd* (Franklin, TN: Providence House Publishers, 2001), 1.

13. Conner, *Christian Doctrine*, 187.

14. Criswell, *Soteriology*, 96.

15. Dagg, *Manual of Theology*, 265–66.

Chapter 8

1. *The Baptist Faith and Message* statement, 11. See Genesis 12:1-3; Exodus 19:5-8; 1 Samuel 8:4-7,19-22; Isaiah 5:1-7; Jeremiah 31:31ff.; Matthew 16:18-19; 21:28-45; 24:22,31; 25:34; Luke 1:68-79; 2:29-32; 19:41-44; 24:44-48; John 1:12-14; 3:16; 5:24; 6:44-45,65; 10:27-29; 15:16; 17:6,12,17-18; Acts 20:32; Romans 5:9-10; 8:28-39; 10:12-15; 11:5-7,26-36; 1 Corinthians 1:1-2; 15:24-28; Ephesians 1:4-23; 2:1-10; 3:1-11; Colossians 1:12-14; 2 Thessalonians 2:13-14; 2 Timothy 1:12; 2:10,19; Hebrews 11:39–12:2; James 1:12; 1 Peter 1:2-5,13; 2:4-10; 1 John 1:7-9; 2:19; 3:2.
2. Eugene H. Peterson, *The Message: The Bible in Contemporary Language* (Colorado Springs: NavPress, 2002), 2126.
3. Hobbs, *The Baptist Faith and Message*, 56.
4. C. H. Spurgeon, *The Metropolitan Tabernacle Pulpit*, vol. 51 (Pasadena, TX: Pilgrim Publications, 1978), 50.
5. Spurgeon, *The New Park Street Pulpit*, vol. 1, 320–21.
6. Dagg, *Manual of Theology*, 316.
7. Mullins, *Baptist Beliefs*, 28.
8. M. E. Dodd, "Once Saved Always Saved," message series, First Baptist Church, Shreveport, Louisiana, 1916) [cited 10 October 2006]. Available from the Internet: *www.elbourne.org/baptist/dodd/index.html*.
9. Dagg, *Manual of Theology*, 298–99.

Chapter 9

1. *The Baptist Faith and Message* statement, 12. See Matthew 16:15-19; 18:15-20; Acts 2:41-42,47; 5:11-14; 6:3-6; 13:1-3; 14:23,27; 15:1-30; 16:5; 20:28; Romans 1:7; 1 Corinthians 1:2; 3:16; 5:4-5; 7:17; 9:13-14; 12; Ephesians 1:22-23; 2:19-22; 3:8-11,21; 5:22-32; Philippians 1:1; Colossians 1:18; 1 Timothy 2:9-14; 3:1-15; 4:14; Hebrews 11:39-40; 1 Peter 5:1-4; Revelation 2–3; 21:2-3.
2. Dodd, *The Democracy of the Saints*, 32.
3. George, *J. M. Frost*, 163.
4. Hobbs, *The Baptist Faith and Message*, 69.

Chapter 10

1. *The Baptist Faith and Message* statement, 13. See Matthew 3:13-17; 26:26-30; 28:19-20; Mark 1:9-11; 14:22-26; Luke 3:21-22; 22:19-20; John 3:23; Acts 2:41-42; 8:35-39; 16:30-33; 20:7; Romans 6:3-5; 1 Corinthians 10:16,21; 11:23-29; Colossians 2:12.
2. L. R. Scarborough, *With Christ After the Lost* (Nashville: Broadman Press, 1952), 271.
3. Adoniram Judson, "Come, Holy Spirit, Dove Divine," in *The Baptist Hymnal*, 364.
4. J. B. Gambrell, *Baptists and Their Business* (Nashville: Sunday School Board Southern Baptist Convention, 1919), 64.

Chapter 11

1. *The Baptist Faith and Message* statement, 14. See Exodus 20:8-11; Matthew 12:1-12; 28:1ff.; Mark 2:27-28; 16:1-7; Luke 24:1-3,33-36; John 4:21-24; 20:1,19-28; Acts 20:7; Romans 14:5-10; 1 Corinthians 16:1-2; Colossians 2:16; 3:16; Revelation 1:10.

Chapter 12

1. *The Baptist Faith and Message* statement, 15. See Genesis 1:1; Isaiah 9:6-7; Jeremiah 23:5-6; Matthew 3:2; 4:8-10,23; 12:25-28; 13:1-52; 25:31-46; 26:29; Mark 1:14-15; 9:1; Luke 4:43; 8:1; 9:2; 12:31-32; 17:20-21; 23:42; John 3:3; 18:36; Acts 1:6-7; 17:22-31; Romans 5:17; 8:19; 1 Corinthians 15:24-28; Colossians 1:13; Hebrews 11:10,16; 12:28; 1 Peter 2:4-10; 4:13; Revelation 1:6,9; 5:10; 11:15; 21–22.

Chapter 13

1. *The Baptist Faith and Message* statement, 15. See Isaiah 2:4; 11:9; Matthew 16:27; 18:8-9; 19:28; 24:27,30,36,44; 25:31-46; 26:64; Mark 8:38; 9:43-48; Luke 12:40,48; 16:19-26; 17:22-37; 21:27-28; John 14:1-3; Acts 1:11; 17:31; Romans 14:10; 1 Corinthians 4:5; 15:24-28,35-58; 2 Corinthians 5:10; Philippians 3:20-21; Colossians 1:5; 3:4; 1 Thessalonians 4:14-18; 5:1ff.; 2 Thessalonians 1:7ff.; 2; 1 Timothy 6:14; 2 Timothy 4:1,8; Titus 2:13; Hebrews 9:27-28; James 5:8; 2 Peter 3:7ff.; 1 John 2:28; 3:2; Jude 14; Revelation 1:18; 3:11; 20:1–22:13.
2. Hobbs, *The Baptist Faith and Message,* 90.
3. David S. Dockery, *Our Christian Hope* (Nashville: LifeWay Press, 1998), 60–61.

Chapter 14

1. *The Baptist Faith and Message* statement, 16. See Genesis 12:1-3; Exodus 19:5-6; Isaiah 6:1-8; Matthew 9:37-38; 10:5-15; 13:18-30,37-43; 16:19; 22:9-10; 24:14; 28:18-20; Luke 10:1-18; 24:46-53; John 14:11-12; 15:7-8,16; 17:15; 20:21; Acts 1:8; 2; 8:26-40; 10:42-48; 13:2-3; Romans 10:13-15; Ephesians 3:1-11; 1 Thessalonians 1:8; 2 Timothy 4:5; Hebrews 2:1-3; 11:39–12:2; 1 Peter 2:4-10; Revelation 22:17.
2. Scarborough, *With Christ After the Lost*, 2.
3. L. R. Scarborough, *After the Resurrection—What?* (Grand Rapids: Zondervan Publishing House, 1942), 74.
4. Henry S. Burrage, *Baptist Hymn Writers and Their Hymns* (Portland, ME: Brown, Thurston, and Co., 1888), 270–71.
5. Thawng Za Lian, e-mail message to Art Criscoe, 19 October 2006.
6. Timothy George, *Faithful Witness: The Life and Mission of William Carey* (Birmingham, AL: New Hope, 1991), 28.

7. Baker James Cauthen, *Beyond Call* (Nashville: Broadman Press, 1973), 44.
8. Louie D. Newton, *Why I Am a Baptist* (New York: Thomas Nelson & Sons, 1957), 228.
9. Jesse C. Fletcher, *Bill Wallace of China* (Nashville: Broadman Press, 1963), 56.
10. Ione Gray, "William Lindsey Wallace," in *Encyclopedia of Southern Baptists*, vol. 2 (Nashville: Broadman Press, 1958), 1475.

Chapter 15

1. *The Baptist Faith and Message* statement, 16–17. See Deuteronomy 4:1,5,9,14; 6:1-10; 31:12-13; Nehemiah 8:1-8; Job 28:28; Psalms 19:7ff.; 119:11; Proverbs 3:13ff.; 4:1-10; 8:1-7,11; 15:14; Ecclesiastes 7:19; Matthew 5:2; 7:24ff.; 28:19-20; Luke 2:40; 1 Corinthians 1:18-31; Ephesians 4:11-16; Philippians 4:8; Colossians 2:3,8-9; 1 Timothy 1:3-7; 2 Timothy 2:15; 3:14-17; Hebrews 5:12–6:3; James 1:5; 3:17.
2. Hobbs, *The Baptist Faith and Message*, 99.

Chapter 16

1. *The Baptist Faith and Message* statement, 17. See Genesis 14:20; Leviticus 27:30-32; Deuteronomy 8:18; Malachi 3:8-12; Matthew 6:1-4,19-21; 19:21; 23:23; 25:14-29; Luke 12:16-21,42; 16:1-13; Acts 2:44-47; 5:1-11; 17:24-25; 20:35; Romans 6:6-22; 12:1-2; 1 Corinthians 4:1-2; 6:19-20; 12; 16:1-4; 2 Corinthians 8–9; 12:15; Philippians 4:10-19; 1 Peter 1:18-19.

Chapter 17

1. *The Baptist Faith and Message* statement, 18. See Exodus 17:12; 18:17ff.; Judges 7:21; Ezra 1:3-4; 2:68-69; 5:14-15; Nehemiah 4; 8:1-5; Matthew 10:5-15; 20:1-16; 22:1-10; 28:19-20; Mark 2:3; Luke 10:1ff.; Acts 1:13-14; 2:1ff.; 4:31-37; 13:2-3; 15:1-35; 1 Corinthians 1:10-17; 3:5-15; 12; 2 Corinthians 8–9; Galatians 1:6-10; Ephesians 4:1-16; Philippians 1:15-18.
2. Daniel, *The Chimes of Shreveport*, 69.
3. Emir and Ergun Caner, *The Sacred Trust: Sketches of the Southern Baptist Convention Presidents* (Nashville: Broadman & Holman Publishers, 2003), 95.
4. R. Earl Allen and Joel Gregory, comps., *Southern Baptist Preaching Yesterday* (Nashville: Broadman Press, 1991), 345.

Chapter 18

1. *The Baptist Faith and Message* statement, 19. See Exodus 20:3-17; Leviticus 6:2-5; Deuteronomy 10:12; 27:17; Psalm 101:5; Micah 6:8; Zechariah 8:16; Matthew 5:13-16, 43-48; 22:36-40; 25:35; Mark 1:29-34; 2:3ff.; 10:21; Luke 4:18-21; 10:27-37; 20:25; John 15:12; 17:15; Romans 12–14; 1 Corinthians 5:9-10; 6:1-7; 7:20-24; 10:23–11:1; Galatians 3:26-28; Ephesians 6:5-9; Colossians 3:12-17; 1 Thessalonians 3:12; Philemon; James 1:27; 2:8.

2. The Southern Baptist Convention has adopted historic resolutions affirming the obligation of all Christians to "contend for the sanctity of all human life, from conception to natural death" and opposing abortion, except to save the mother's life (SBC 1979, 1982, 1984).
3. M. E. Dodd, as quoted by Caner, *The Sacred Trust*, 77–78.

Chapter 19

1. *The Baptist Faith and Message* statement, 20. See Isaiah 2:4; Matthew 5:9,38-48; 6:33; 26:52; Luke 22:36,38; Romans 12:18-19; 13:1-7; 14:19; Hebrews 12:14; James 4:1-2.

Chapter 20

1. *The Baptist Faith and Message* statement, 20–21. See Genesis 1:27; 2:7; Matthew 6:6-7,24; 16:26; 22:21; John 8:36; Acts 4:19-20; Romans 6:1-2; 13:1-7; Galatians 5:1,13; Philippians 3:20; 1 Timothy 2:1-2; James 4:12; 1 Peter 2:12-17; 3:11-17; 4:12-19.
2. Hobbs, *The Baptist Faith and Message*, 121.
3. Judson Boyce Allen, "Obadiah Holmes," in *Encyclopedia of Southern Baptists*, vol. 2 (Nashville: Broadman Press, 1958), 629–30.
4. H. Leon McBeth, *The Baptist Heritage* (Nashville: Broadman Press, 1987), 139–40.
5. Timothy and Denise George, eds., *James P. Boyce: Treasures from the Baptist Heritage* (Nashville: Broadman & Holman Publishers, 1996), 241–42.
6. Ibid., 244.
7. Gambrell, *Baptists and Their Business*, 144.
8. Ergun Caner and Emir Caner, eds., *The Sacred Desk: Sermons of the Southern Baptist Convention Presidents* (Nashville: Broadman & Holman Publishers, 2004), 159.
9. H. Leon McBeth, *A Sourcebook for Baptist Heritage* (Nashville: Broadman Press, 1990), 179.
10. William L. Lumpkin, *Baptist Confessions of Faith* (Valley Forge, PA: Judson Press, 1959), 140.
11. McBeth, *The Baptist Heritage*, 32.
12. Mohler, comp., *E. Y. Mullins*, 275.
13. McBeth, *A Sourcebook for Baptist Heritage*, 72.
14. Mohler, comp., *E. Y. Mullins*, 80.

Chapter 21

1. *The Baptist Faith and Message* statement, 21–22. See Genesis 1:26-28; 2:15-25; 3:1-20; Exodus 20:12; Deuteronomy 6:4-9; Joshua 24:15; 1 Samuel 1:26-28; Psalms 51:5; 78:1-8; 127; 128; 139:13-16; Proverbs 1:8; 5:15-20; 6:20-22; 12:4; 13:24; 14:1; 17:6; 18:22; 22:6,15; 23:13-14; 24:3; 29:15,17; 31:10-31; Ecclesiastes 4:9-12; 9:9; Malachi 2:14-16; Matthew 5:31-32; 18:2-5; 19:3-9; Mark 10:6-12; Romans 1:18-32; 1 Corinthians 7:1-16; Ephesians 5:21-33; 6:1-4; Colossians 3:18-21; 1 Timothy 5:8,14; 2 Timothy 1:3-5; Titus 2:3-5; Hebrews 13:4; 1 Peter 3:1-7.

LEADER GUIDE

This guide provides suggestions for leading a small-group study of this book. After completing this study, participants should be able to—

- articulate basic Baptist beliefs;
- give the biblical foundation for these beliefs;
- apply the beliefs to their Christian walks.

The teaching suggestions call for a high degree of member involvement. Participants will share their experiences, study Scriptures together, and complete a variety of learning activities to help them understand the doctrines being studied and apply biblical truth to their lives. Your job is to serve as a guide and facilitator.

Advance Planning

1. Schedule a minimum of six 1½-hour sessions for this study.
2. Promote the study.
3. Order a copy of this book (item 005035536) for each participant. Distribute the books in advance and ask members to read chapter 1 and to complete the learning activities before the first group session.
4. Order a supply of *The Baptist Faith and Message* tract (item 001146686).
5. Read the entire leader guide several weeks before the first session. Many sentence strips, placards, signs, and teaching posters are called for. You can make the visuals by hand, using poster board or large sheets of paper and felt-tip markers. Paper adding-machine tape makes excellent sentence strips. You can make PowerPoint® slides of all visuals to project during the sessions. Or you can make overhead cels of the visuals and use an overhead projector.
6. Gather all of the resources you will need. In addition to the visuals, you will need three-by-five-inch cards; masking tape; copies of *The Baptist Hymnal*; a dictionary; a large, light-colored ball about 15 inches in diameter; 15 to 20 boxes of various sizes to represent spiritual gifts; gift-wrapping paper and ribbon; a salt-shaker; a candle; and matches.

7. Prepare a course poster to use in each session:

   Session 1: *The Scriptures*

   Session 2: *God, God the Father, God the Son, God the Holy Spirit*

   Session 3: *Man, Salvation, God's Purpose of Grace*

   Session 4: *The Church, Baptism and the Lord's Supper, The Lord's Day, The Kingdom, Last Things*

   Session 5: *Evangelism and Missions, Education, Stewardship, Cooperation*

   Session 6: *The Christian and the Social Order, Peace and War, Religious Liberty, The Family*

8. There is no substitute for prayerful, intensive study and preparation. Reading the entire book several times will give you a good foundation for teaching. Read all of the Scripture references in the book and complete all of the learning activities. Jot down teaching ideas. This preparation will allow you to lead and teach from an overflow of knowledge.

Planning for Each Session

1. Study in detail the chapter or chapters for the session, along with the teaching plans. You will probably find more teaching suggestions than you will have time to use during the session. Select the activities that will best meet the needs of your group.

2. Prepare visual aids and other materials you will need for the session.

3. The teaching posters for each session create an attractive room environment, allow learning to begin as soon as the first person arrives, reinforce learning, and provide review. Mount the posters in random order and at various angles around the room to attract attention.

4. Arrange seating in a circle or a semicircle so that members can see one another.

Leading Each Session

1. Arrive early to greet members as they arrive. Start and stop on time. Begin and close each session with prayer.

2. Encourage members to read the assigned chapters and to complete the learning activities before each group session.

3. Suggestions in this guide call for dividing into five small groups from time to time. The ideal small-group size for this study is three persons. If there are not enough members for five groups, combine some of the assignments. If there are more than enough members for five groups, divide into more groups and give duplicate assignments.

4. Be sensitive to the needs of the group. Be flexible and adapt your teaching plans as needed. However, do not allow the discussion to wander. Keep the focus on the subject at hand.

5. Do not talk too much. Involve members in the learning process by encouraging

them to share their insights, questions, and feelings. Do not be afraid of silence.

6. Magnify the Bible as our source of authority.

Session 1
The Scriptures

Before the Session

1. Study chapter 1. Complete the activities.
2. Prepare teaching posters and display them around the room: *The Bible is God's revelation of Himself to us. The Bible is to be trusted and obeyed. The Bible is the sure foundation on which to build our lives. God always has something fresh for us in His Word. Jesus is the ultimate focus of every verse of Scripture.*
3. Prepare placards with the terms *general revelation* and *special revelation.*
4. Write agree/disagree statements on a large sheet of paper: *1. God's revelation of Himself is confined to the Bible. 2. The revelation of God we have in nature is sufficient to save people if they are obedient. 3. God dictated the exact words He wanted recorded in Scripture. 4. Some parts of the Bible are more inspired than others. 5. The Bible contains no errors of any kind.*
5. Prepare sentence strips: *God is its Author. Salvation is its purpose. It is truth without any mixture of error.*
6. Write the following Scripture references on separate three-by-five-inch cards: Card 1: *Psalm 19:7-10.* Card 2: *Psalm 119:11,89,105,140.* Card 3: *2 Timothy*

3:16-17. Card 4: *1 Peter 1:24-25.* Card 5: *2 Peter 1:19-21.*

7. Prepare placards: *Theories of Inspiration, Dynamic Theory, Dictation Theory, Verbal Plenary Theory.*
8. Write the following questions on separate three-by-five-inch cards: *How can we be sure the Bible is God's Word? How can we be sure God inspired the Bible? What does it mean to say the Bible is inspired? How would you explain to a person who has never seen the Bible that it is God's Word? What are some ways we can demonstrate our love for the Bible?*
9. Provide a dictionary and copies of *The Baptist Hymnal.*

During the Session

1. Greet everyone. Make sure everyone has a copy of the book.
2. Write the word *doctrine* on the board. Ask: *What do you think of when you hear this word?* Write responses on the board. Ask a volunteer to read the definition from the dictionary. Point out that the word *doctrine* comes from a root Greek verb meaning *to teach.* Doctrine is what is taught or teaching. Ask: *Why is doctrine important?* After responses share: *Doctrine provides a foundation for our Christian lives, provides principles for us to live by, equips us to reject false teaching, helps us grow toward Christian maturity, and prepares us to serve God with our whole minds.*

3. Using the course poster, point out the various doctrines to be studied. Lead in prayer, asking God to reveal the truth of His Word as you study together.

4. State that this session focuses on the Scriptures. Show the agree/disagree statements. Read a statement and, by a show of hands, determine who agrees, who disagrees, and who is undecided. If the group is divided, allow time for brief discussion. Answers: 1. D; 2. D (Paul asserted in Rom. 1 that no one is obedient.); 3. D (We have the exact words God wanted recorded in Scripture, but He did not dictate them to passive writers.) 4. D; 5. A.

5. Display the two placards *General Revelation* and *Special Revelation*. Define each type of revelation. Read the following and ask members to name the type of revelation it represents: *a flower, Genesis 1:1, a field of grain, a sunset, Leviticus, the conscience, a storm, Christ's birth, a river, John 3:16.*

6. Distribute copies of *The Baptist Hymnal*. Ask two volunteers to read stanzas 1 and 2 of *How Great Thou Art* (no. 10). Ask: *What kind of revelation do these stanzas refer to?* Then ask a volunteer to read stanza 3. Ask, *What kind of revelation does this stanza refer to?*

7. Ask a volunteer to read Psalm 19:1-4. Ask members to describe times when they were drawn close to God through His creation. Point out that general revelation is not enough. We could look at a beautiful sunset every day for a hundred years and still never know God's name, nor would we learn of Christ's coming or His death on the cross. That is why God has given us special revelation, the Bible.

8. Display the sentence strip *God is its Author.* Then display the placards with the theories of inspiration. Briefly explain the three theories.

9. Call for responses to the matching activity on page 11 and to the true/false activity on page 12.

10. Display the sentence strip *Salvation is its purpose.* Summarize the section "Salvation for Its End," beginning on page 13. Point out that the main purpose of the Bible is to point us to Jesus Christ and tell us how to be saved.

11. Display the sentence strip *It is truth without any mixture of error.* Share the story of Billy Graham (pp. 15–16).

12. Write *authoritative, infallible, inerrant, sufficient,* and *eternal* on the board. Ask members to define them. Share the account from Jeremiah 36 (p. 19).

13. Divide into five small groups and give each group one of the cards with Scripture references. Ask each group to study its Scripture, discuss what it means, and report to the large group. Allow time for work and call for reports.

14. Give each of the five groups one of the cards with questions. Ask the groups to discuss the questions and report to

the large group how they would answer. Allow time for work and call for reports.

15. Review the three main points of the session, using the sentence strips. Ask members to work in pairs, taking turns briefly sharing what Baptists believe about the Bible.

16. State that one of the greatest ways we can show our love for God's Word is to read it every day. Call attention to the prayer of commitment to read the Bible every day (margin, p. 20). Sign the commitment and encourage members to sign also.

17. Call attention to the teaching posters on the walls. Ask volunteers to read them and comment on their meanings.

18. Explain that God has promised to bless us when we meditate on His Word. Introduce members to the ancient biblical practice of meditation by reviewing the guidelines in the activity on page 20. Call attention to the memory verses for this session, 2 Timothy 3:16-17. Challenge members to meditate on this passage each day this week.

19. Ask members to read chapters 2–5 and to complete the activities before the next session.

20. Read or sing "Break Thou the Bread of Life" (The Baptist Hymnal, no. 263) as a closing prayer.

Session 2
God, God the Father, God the Son, God the Holy Spirit

Before the Session

1. Study chapters 2–5. Complete the activities.
2. Prepare teaching posters and display them around the room: *God is in charge of the universe. God knows the name on your mailbox. Jesus Christ is the eternal Son of God. Christ died in our place. The Holy Spirit dwells in every believer. The Holy Spirit helps us understand truth.*
3. Prepare signs with these outlines:

God

Creator	Providence
Redeemer	Omnipotence
Preserver	Omniscience
Ruler	Love
The Trinity	

Jesus Christ

Preexistence	Death
Birth	Resurrection
Life	Return

The Holy Spirit

Inspired Scripture	Regenerates
Teaches, guides	Dwells in believers
Convicts of sin	Bestows gifts
Invites to Christ	Seals believers
Illuminates truth	Intercedes for believers
Builds the church	

4. Write the following Scripture references on separate three-by-five-inch cards: Card 1: *Ephesians 1:13-14; John 14:16-17.* Card 2: *Ephesians 4:7-8; John 16:7-11.* Card 3: *John 3:5-6; 1 Corinthians 6:19.* Card 4: *Titus 3:5-6; John 14:26; 1 Corinthians 2:13.* Card 5: *1 Corinthians 3:16; John 16:13-14; Ephesians 4:30.*

5. Provide copies of *The Baptist Hymnal.*

During the Session

1. Distribute copies of *The Baptist Hymnal.* Ask two volunteers to read the first two stanzas of "Open My Eyes, That I May See" (no. 502) as a prayer. Or lead the group in singing the hymn as a prayer.

2. Use the course poster to point out the topics of study for this session.

3. Direct attention to the matching activity on page 24. Complete the activity as a group. Allow time for discussion of God's attributes.

4. Display the sign *God* and summarize the points. When you get to *The Trinity,* direct attention to the true/false activity on the Trinity, page 28. Involve members in discussing the statements.

5. When you get to *Providence,* summarize the accounts of Joseph (see Gen. 50:15-21) and Elijah (see 1 Kings 17:2-7), using the activities on pages 32–33. Direct attention to the activity on Matthew 6:25-34, page 33. Ask a volunteer to read the passage as members complete the activity.

6. Display the sign *Jesus Christ* and lead the group to discuss the points. Under *Life* read R. G. Lee's contrast of Jesus' humanity and deity (p. 42).

7. Explain that catechisms, short question-and-answer documents about Christianity, were widely used by the early church and later by early Baptists. Ask members to turn to *The Baptist Faith and Message* article on God the Son, page 39. Ask the questions in the activity on page 50 as members answer, based on the article.

8. Display the sign *The Holy Spirit* and lead the group to discuss the points. Then call for responses to the true/false statements on the Holy Spirit, page 56.

9. Divide into five small groups and give each group a card with Scripture references. Ask each group to study its verses and report on what they teach about the Holy Spirit's ministry.

10. Ask members to summarize the session by reading aloud meaningful statements from the posters on the walls.

11. Ask whether any members would like to share testimonies about their times of meditation last week. Call attention to the four memory passages for this week: Exodus 20:3; Matthew 6:26; Romans 5:8; and Ephesians 5:18. Encourage members to continue their meditation, using these verses.

12. Ask members to read chapters 6–8 and to complete the activities before the next session.

13. Ask members to reflect on the self-evaluation on page 58. Read or sing "Breathe on Me" (*The Baptist Hymnal*, p. 238) as a closing prayer.

Session 3
Man, Salvation, God's Purpose of Grace

Before the Session

1. Study chapters 6–8. Complete the activities.
2. Prepare teaching posters and display them around the room: *We are made in God's image. We are sinners by nature and sinners by choice. The cross stands at the very center of the Christian faith. "Everyone who calls on the name of the Lord will be saved" (Rom. 10:13). Repentance is godly sorrow for sin and turning away from it. Our salvation is secure in Christ.*
3. Write the following agree/disagree statements on a large sheet of paper: 1. *We are born in a state of moral innocence. 2. The basic human problem is ignorance, not sin. 3. Christ died as our example. 4. Jesus Christ is the only way to heaven. 5. Man does not possess free will. 6. It is possible for Christians to lose their salvation.*
4. Write the following Scripture references on separate three-by-five-inch cards: Card 1: *Genesis 1:26-27; 2:7.* Card 2: *Genesis 9:6; James 3:9.* Card 3: *Psalm 51:5; Romans 3:10-12,23; 5:12.* Card 4: *John 3:16; Romans 5:6-8.* Card 5: *2 Corinthians 5:21; 1 Timothy 2:5.*
5. Prepare separate slips of paper with the following Scripture references: *Romans 5:8-9; Ephesians 1:7; Ephesians 2:13; 1 Peter 1:18-19; 1 John 1:7; Revelation 1:5.*
6. Prepare a sign with the terms *regeneration, justification, sanctification, glorification.*
7. Prepare this acrostic on poster board:
   God's
   Riches
   At
   Christ's
   Expense
8. Cut a large circle from poster board. Write *repentance* on one side and *faith* on the other side.
9. Write the following Scripture references on separate three-by-five-inch cards: Card 1: *2 Timothy 1:12; Philippians 1:6.* Card 2: *Hebrews 7:25.* Card 3: *John 5:24.* Card 4: *1 Peter 1:3-5.* Card 5: *Hebrews 13:5.*

During the Session

1. Use the course poster to point out the topics of study for this session. Ask a volunteer to lead in prayer.
2. Show the agree/disagree statements. Read the first statement and ask members who agree with it to raise their hands. Then ask those who disagree to raise their hands. Then determine who is undecided. Allow time for discussion. Follow this pattern for the other statements. *Disagree* is the correct response for all of the statements except number 4, which is *agree.*

183

State that this session will make clear the correct responses.

3. Call attention to the true/false activity on page 61. Use these statements as the basis for discussion.

4. Divide into five small groups and give each group one of the first set of cards with Scripture references. Ask each group to study its passages and to summarize what they teach about humanity. Allow time for group work and call for reports. Allow time for discussion as reports are shared.

5. Direct attention to the true/false activity on page 67. Lead the group to respond to and discuss the statements.

6. Hand out the slips of paper with Scripture references. Write the word *atonement* on the board. Ask members to locate and read their verse or verses. Make clear that Christ shed His blood for our sins. Circle the word *atonement* and say that this term refers to the way God dealt with the problem of sin and made it possible for us to enter fellowship with Him. We are saved through Christ's death on the cross.

7. Display the sign with the terms *regeneration, justification, sanctification,* and *glorification*. Direct attention to *The Baptist Faith and Message* article on salvation (p. 65). Ask a volunteer to read the section on *regeneration*. Lead a discussion of the meaning of *grace*. Display the acrostic that defines *grace*.

8. Display the large circle showing the word *repentance*. Read its definition from *The Baptist Faith and Message* statement. Then turn the circle over and show the word *faith*. Read its definition from *The Baptist Faith and Message* article. Point out that repentance and faith are like two sides of the same coin; they go together. Read the quotation by W. T. Conner emphasizing the relationship between repentance and faith (pp. 72–73).

9. Ask three volunteers to read *The Baptist Faith and Message* paragraphs on *justification, sanctification,* and *glorification*. Lead a discussion of these three concepts. Allow time for questions.

10. Refer to the matching activity on page 76 on *regeneration, justification, sanctification,* and *glorification*. Make sure the terms are understood.

11. Display the circle poster again and ask volunteers to define the terms *repentance* and *faith*.

12. Referring to chapter 8, summarize the material on election. Lead in discussing the topics of God's sovereignty and humanity's free will.

13. Introduce the security of the believer by asking members to turn to Romans 8:38-39 and name 10 things that cannot separate us from God's love.

14. Divide into five small groups and give each group one of the second set of cards. Ask each group to examine what the verse or verses teach about the

security of the believer. Allow time for group work and then call for reports.

15. Call attention to the true/false activity on page 84. Discuss the statements. Ask members to select and read aloud teaching posters on the walls.

16. Ask for testimonies from members' times of meditation. Challenge members to use the memory passages for this week, Genesis 1:27; John 3:16; and John 10:27-29, for their meditation.

17. Ask members to read chapters 9–13 and to complete the activities before the next session.

18. Close by singing the first two stanzas of "I Know Whom I Have Believed" (The Baptist Hymnal, no. 337).

Session 4
The Church, Baptism and the Lord's Supper, The Lord's Day, The Kingdom, Last Things

Before the Session

1. Study chapter 9–13. Complete the activities.

2. Prepare teaching posters and display them around the room: *Jesus Christ is Lord of His church. Baptism and the Lord's Supper teach basic truths of the gospel. The Lord's Day commemorates Christ's resurrection. The kingdom of God is eternal. A person's eternal destiny is decided in this life. Jesus will come back to earth.*

3. Use one-inch masking tape to outline a large human body, about 20 to 25 feet long, on the floor. Make the body large enough for 10 to 12 persons to stand inside it. The midsection should be about three feet across, the legs about one foot across, and the arms slightly smaller.

4. Wrap 15 to 20 boxes of various sizes to represent spiritual gifts.

5. Write the following Scripture references on separate three-by-five-inch cards: Card 1: *Matthew 16:13-19.* Card 2: *Acts 6:1-3.* Card 3: *Ephesians 2:19-22.* Card 4: *Colossians 1:17-18.* Card 5: *1 Peter 5:1-4.*

6. Write the following questions or statements on separate assignment slips: *In what way is the church the body of Christ? Who is the head of the church? What are the two ordinances of the church? What is the primary mission of the church? How can our church witness to the ends of the earth? How does our church relate to the local association? How does our church relate to the Baptist state convention? How does our church relate to the Southern Baptist Convention? How does our church relate to the International Mission Board? What I like best about our church is … One thing I would like to change about our church is … One way I can help strengthen our church is … State in one sentence what the church means to you.*

7. Write the following Scripture references on separate three-by-five-inch cards: Card 1: *Matthew 24:36-44.* Card 2: *Luke*

185

12:8-9. Card 3: *John 5:28-29.* Card 4: *Acts 1:9-11.* Card 5: *Revelation 20:11-15.*

8. Enlist three members to complete the following assignments. Assignment 1: *Study the material on heaven on pages 117–18 and Revelation 21–22. Give a brief report during the session.* Assignment 2: *Study the material on hell on pages 118–19 and Luke 16:19-31. Give a brief report during the session.* Assignment 3: *Study the topic "The Final Judgment" on pages 119–20 and Revelation 20:11-15. Give a brief report during the session.*

9. Bring to the session one communion cup with grape juice and one small piece of communion bread.

During the Session

1. Use the course poster to show the topics for this session. Lead in prayer.

2. Explain that Paul used the analogy of the human body to describe the church as the body of Christ. Direct attention to the large body outlined on the floor and state that it represents the body of Christ. Ask a member to read 1 Corinthians 12:12-27. Tell the group that you and seven or eight members will illustrate this passage. You will represent the Holy Spirit. Go to a member and lead him to a place in the body. Then place a gift box in his hands. Lead the other persons, one at a time, to positions in the outline. Do not place anyone in the head. Give several members two gift boxes, one person

three gift boxes, and another four gift boxes. As these persons stand in position, ask the other members to turn to the first activity on page 87. Ask volunteers to read the seven points listed in the activity. Allow time for discussion. Ask, What is wrong with the persons standing in the body? Point out that each person has received at least one gift; yet the gifts are unopened. This is often true in the church. Each believer has received gifts from the Holy Spirit, but sometimes the gifts are not used.[1]

3. Divide into five small groups and distribute the first set of cards with Scripture references. Ask each group to study its assigned Scripture, discuss what it teaches about the church, and report to the large group. Allow time for group work and call for reports.

4. Direct attention to the true/false activity on page 92. Lead the group to respond to and discuss the statements.

5. Distribute the assignment slips and ask members who received them to answer the questions. Discuss as needed.

6. Call attention to the two ordinances of the church. Read *The Baptist Faith and Message* article on baptism (p. 93). Write on the board: *While baptism is not necessary for salvation, it is necessary for obedience.* Ask, *What does this statement mean?* Allow time for discussion.

7. Summarize what Baptists believe about baptism by leading the group in the true/false activity on page 95.

8. Display the communion cup of juice and the piece of communion bread. Read *The Baptist Faith and Message* article on the Lord's Supper (p. 93). Summarize the material on the Lord's Supper, pages 97–99.

9. Call for answers to the true/false activity on page 99. Allow discussion.

10. Ask a volunteer to read *The Baptist Faith and Message* article on the Lord's Day (p. 101). Use the two activities on page 104 to summarize our beliefs.

11. Ask, *How do you determine the kinds of activities you engage in on the Lord's Day?* Point out the four main elements of corporate worship on page 106 (preaching, songs and hymns, Scripture reading, prayer) and the three main elements of private devotion on page 106 (Scripture reading, prayer, Christian service).

12. Summarize the material on the kingdom of God, page 108, by contrasting God's kingdom with earthly kingdoms. Call for responses to the activity on page 109.

13. Read the 10 statements on the kingdom in the activity on pages 110–11.

14. Ask a volunteer to read *The Baptist Faith and Message* article on Last Things (p. 113). Ask members to listen for four things that will take place when Christ returns. Discuss these.

15. Divide into five small groups and give each group one of the second set of cards with Scripture references. Ask each group to study the assigned Scripture and discuss what it means. Allow time for group work and call for reports.

16. Call on the members enlisted to report on heaven, hell, and final judgment. Allow questions and discussion.

17. Call for responses to the true/false activity on page 120.

18. Ask, *What is one new thing you have learned in this session?* Allow discussion.

19. Summarize by asking volunteers to read the teaching posters on the walls.

20. Challenge members to meditate on their memory verses this week: Colossians 1:18; 2 Corinthians 5:17; Psalm 122:1; Matthew 6:33; John 14:1-3.

21. Ask members to read chapters 14–17 and to complete the activities before the next session. Close with prayer.

1. This idea came from an activity developed by Ray Stedman and the staff of Peninsula Bible Church in Palo Alto, California.

Session 5
Evangelism and Missions, Education, Stewardship, Cooperation

Before the Session

1. Study chapters 14–17. Complete the activities.

2. Prepare teaching posters and display them around the room: *Christians are responsible to take the gospel to every person in the world. Christianity is the faith*

of enlightenment and intelligence. Education undergirds evangelism and missions. God owns everything. Churches can do together what no one church could do alone.

3. Write the following Scripture references on separate three-by-five-inch cards: Card 1: *Matthew 28:19-20.* Card 2: *1 Corinthians 1:30.* Card 3: *Ephesians 4:11-13.* Card 4: *Philippians 4:8.* Card 5: *2 Timothy 2:15.*

4. Write the following Scripture references on separate three-by-five-inch cards: Card 1: *Matthew 6:1-4,19-21.* Card 2: *Matthew 23:23; Acts 17:24.* Card 3: *Luke 12:16-21.* Card 4: *Acts 20:35; 2 Corinthians 9:7.* Card 5: *Philippians 4:11-13; 1 Peter 1:18-19.*

5. Find out how much money or what percentage of income your church gives to the Lord's work through the Cooperative Program.

During the Session

1. Use the course poster to point out the topics of study for this session. Lead in prayer.

2. Use the teaching posters on the walls to overview the session. Ask volunteers to select a poster, read it to the group, and explain it in their own words.

3. Use the questions in the activity on page 124 as the basis for a discussion of missions.

4. Tell the story of Adoniram Judson and describe the way his legacy continues today in Myanmar (p. 124).

5. Direct members to the matching activity on page 126. Ask five volunteers to read the Scripture passages as the group selects the statement that summarizes the main teachings.

6. Introduce education by asking, *What do the 27 books and letters of the New Testament imply about the teaching ministry of the early church?* (The early church was concerned about helping believers understand the Christian faith and grow in Christian maturity.)

7. Divide into five small groups and give each group one of the first set of cards. Ask each group to study its Scripture passage and summarize what it says about education and teaching. Allow time for group work and call for reports.

8. Use the statements in the activity on page 133 to show the way education undergirds evangelism and missions.

9. Introduce stewardship by reading *The Baptist Faith and Message* article, page 135.

10. Ask a volunteer to read Matthew 6:19-21. Ask: *What are some treasures that people collect on earth? How do people collect treasures on earth? What happens to treasures collected on earth? What are some ways a Christian can collect treasures in heaven?* (Some examples are listed in the activity on p. 137.) *What happens to treasures collected in heaven? What does verse 21 mean?*

11. Divide into the same five groups formed earlier and give each group one of the second set of cards with

Scripture references. Ask each group to study its passage and summarize what it says about stewardship. Allow time for group work and call for reports.

12. Ask two volunteers to help with a role play. Both players are Christians, but one strongly believes that a Christian should not tithe. The other believes just as strongly that every Christian should tithe. Divide the rest of the group into two teams to support the two Christians. No one is allowed to speak except the two players, but each team can help its player by whispering comments to the player or by writing comments on slips of paper and handing them to the player. After a few minutes summarize the material on pages 139–40.

13. Emphasize that stewardship involves much more than material possessions. Ask members to bow their heads as you identify some assets that God gives to every Christian. Ask members to think of one way they can be better stewards of each asset. Slowly read: *body, mind, abilities, time, influence, spiritual gifts.*

14. Introduce cooperation by asking four volunteers to read the following Scripture passages: Ezra 1:1-4; Mark 2:3-4; Acts 2:44-47; 1 Corinthians 16:1-4. Ask the group to identify the kind of cooperation represented in each passage.

15. Write the following two statements on the board: *Baptists believe in voluntary association. Congregationalism is a deeply established Baptist principle.* Lead the group to discuss the meaning of each statement (see p. 143).

16. Summarize the information about the Cooperative Program. Share information about your church's giving through the Cooperative Program.

17. Challenge members to continue with their meditation on Scripture. Verses for this week are Romans 10:13-15; Psalm 25:4-5; Matthew 6:19-21; 1 Corinthians 3:9.

18. Ask members to read chapters 18–21 and to complete the activities before the next session.

19. Close with prayer for world missions.

Session 6
The Christian and the Social Order, Peace and War, Religious Liberty, The Family

Before the Session

1. Study chapters 18–21. Complete the activities.

2. Prepare teaching posters and display them around the room: *Churches should reach out to the less fortunate. Racism is a sin that violates the character of God and the unity of humankind, which is made in God's image. Churches should minister to persons struggling with homosexuality. All human life is sacred from conception to natural death. War is the result of human sinfulness. Marriage is the uniting of one man and one woman in covenant commit-*

ment for a lifetime. The family is a central part of God's design for humanity.

3. Write the following Scripture references on separate three-by-five-inch cards: Card 1: *Romans 13:1-7.* Card 2: *1 Timothy 2:1-2.* Card 3: *1 Peter 2:13-17.*

4. Prepare separate slips of paper with these Scripture references: *1 Timothy 3:16-17; Hebrews 4:12; Deuteronomy 6:4; Matthew 6:26; John 1:1; John 14:6; John 14:16-17; 1 Corinthians 6:19; Genesis 2:7; Psalm 8:3-8; Romans 10:13; Ephesians 2:8; Philippians 1:6; John 10:28.*

5. Obtain a saltshaker, a candle, matches, and copies of *The Baptist Faith and Message* tract.

During the Session

1. Display the course poster and call attention to the four topics of study for this session. Ask a member to pray.

2. Introduce the Christian and the social order by displaying the saltshaker and the candle. Light the candle. Ask, *What did Jesus mean when He said we are to be salt and light?* Use Matthew 5:13-16 to discuss these two metaphors.

3. Write the following terms on the board: *racism, homosexuality, abortion, people in need, the sick, the poor, war.* State: *Christians are called to become involved in contemporary issues and problems as salt and light.* Ask members to locate a poster that addresses racism. Ask a volunteer to explain why racism is a sin. Then ask members to identify posters that speak to homosexuality, abortion, people in need, and war. Ask members to explain and discuss the meaning of each poster. Ask: *What are some actions Christians can take to deal with each issue?* Allow time for discussion.

4. Introduce religious liberty by telling the story of Obadiah Holmes (pp. 162–63). Ask, What does Herschel Hobbs's statement mean: "Religious liberty is the mother of all true freedom"?

5. Ask volunteers to read the quotations by George Truett, John Leland, J. B. Gambrell, Louie D. Newton, E. Y. Mullins, John Smyth, and Thomas Helwys (pp. 163–65).

6. Hand out to three members the cards you prepared. As the Scripture passages are read, ask the group to listen for at least four responsibilities we have toward civil government. Write them on the board as they are named. Allow time for discussion.

7. Introduce the family by asking members to identify two teaching posters on the walls that relate to family. Remove them from the walls and attach them to the board, where everyone can easily see them. Ask these questions about each statement: *What does this statement mean? How is modern culture challenging the truth of this statement? Why do you think it is important that Christians emphasize the truth of this statement? What are some actions our church can take to uphold and reinforce*

the truth of this statement? Use the last two questions as thought questions only: *What can I personally do to apply this truth more consistently in my life and in my family? How can I strengthen my marriage and my family?*

8. Refer members to *The Baptist Faith and Message* article on the family (p. 167). Ask them to listen for four purposes of marriage as you read the second paragraph of the statement. Write the purposes on the board.

9. To review the entire study, hand out the 14 slips of paper. State that these 14 Scripture passages relate to seven of the doctrines we have studied, two Scripture passages for each doctrine. Display the course poster. Ask each person to read the Scripture passage and to find the person who has a passage on the same doctrine. Then ask each pair to read its passages aloud, identify the doctrine to which they refer, and share some things they have learned about that doctrine. (The seven sets of Scripture passages deal with the Bible, God, Jesus Christ, the Holy Spirit, man, salvation, and God's purpose of grace.) Give the other group members the opportunity to contribute.

10. Call attention to the other 13 topics on the course poster. Give members the opportunity to share some things they have learned about each topic.

11. Give each member a copy of *The Baptist Faith and Message* tract.

12. Write on the board the Scripture references for this week's meditation: Matthew 5:14-16; Romans 12:18; 1 Timothy 2:1-2; Ephesians 4:32.

13. Thank members for their participation. Close the study with prayer.

Two Ways to Earn Credit
for Studying LifeWay Christian Resources Material

Christian Growth Study Plan resources are available for course credit for personal growth and church leadership training.

Courses are designed as plans for personal spiritual growth and for training current and future church leaders. To receive credit, complete the book, material, or activity. Respond to the learning activities or attend group sessions, when applicable, and show your work to your pastor, staff member, or church leader. Then go to *www.lifeway.com/CGSP*, or call the toll-free number for instructions for receiving credit and your certificate of completion.

For information about studies in the Christian Growth Study Plan, refer to the current catalog online at the CGSP Web address. This program and certificate are free LifeWay services to you.

CONTACT INFORMATION:
Christian Growth Study Plan
One LifeWay Plaza, MSN 117
Nashville, TN 37234
CGSP info line 1-800-968-5519
www.lifeway.com/CGSP
To order resources 1-800-458-2772

Need a CEU?

Receive Continuing Education Units (CEUs) when you complete group Bible studies by your favorite LifeWay authors.

Some studies are approved by the Association of Christian Schools International (ACSI) for CEU credits. Do you need to renew your Christian school teaching certificate? Gather a group of teachers or neighbors and complete one of the approved studies. Then go to *www.lifeway.com/CEU* to submit a request form or to find a list of ACSI-approved LifeWay studies and conferences. Book studies must be completed in a group setting. Online courses approved for ACSI credit are also noted on the course list. The administrative cost of each CEU certificate is only $10 per course.

CONTACT INFORMATION:
CEU Coordinator
One LifeWay Plaza, MSN 150
Nashville, TN 37234
Info line 1-800-968-5519
www.lifeway.com/CEU